Horizon

AUTUMN, 1968 · VOLUME X, NUMBER 4

Our Authors: Right or Wrong?

Much as we admire the authors of certain articles in this issue, we must differ with some of their conclusions. Roy McMullen, who writes with such obvious enjoyment of Gaudí's architecture, nevertheless ends up with the dictum that, for all his genius, one Gaudí was enough for the world. Why? Evidently because his two apartment houses, with their dim rooms and undulating walls, might be a little spooky to live in. This is essentially the criticism made of Gaudí by the followers of the international modern, or Bauhaus, school, which has come to dominate the architectural world in this century.

The high priest of the functional modern school is Mies van der Rohe, and his temple is the Seagram Building on Park Avenue. It is indeed an architectural landmark—perhaps as great in its way as Gaudí's cathedral of the Sagrada Família. And whereas Gaudí had no direct followers, Mies is the most widely imitated of architects. One has only to look up and down Park Avenue from the Seagram Building to see the dreary results. Block after block, the steel-and-glass boxes seem to proclaim: "One Mies would have been enough."

No one would want to see a landscape entirely filled with buildings designed by lesser Gaudís. But a few more exotic architects, following their own imaginations instead of the gospel that "less is more," would relieve the deadly monotony of modern "functional" architecture.

As for functionalism, what is the function of a park or a cathedral? Not, surely, the same as that of a kitchen or an office. A park is to delight; a cathedral is to inspire. In these, his major works, Gaudí was triumphantly successful.

Sagrada Família   *Seagram Building*

The presence—or absence—of genius in our society concerns Edmund Stillman also, in his provocative article "Before the Fall." Among the great philosophers of history Mr. Stillman finds some agreement that one symptom of decline in a civilization is the failure of creativity. When a society ceases to produce new ideas and talents—when it turns to critical analysis of its own cul-

Horizon

A Magazine of the Arts

AUTUMN, 1968 · VOLUME X, NUMBER 4

ture and begins to draw its fresh ideas from its own lowest classes or the "outside" world—then that society has passed from its phase of youthful vitality to one of repression and sterility.

It is not hard to find such symptoms in our society. The loss of faith in goals our fathers took for granted, the frantic search for this year's new sensation in the arts, the adoption by the "ruling elite" of styles that originated in the slums, the turning away from established religion to drugs and swamis—all these fit the Toynbeean pattern of cultural decline. They seem, in Gilbert Murray's phrase, to mark a "failure of nerve."

And yet, who can say that out of the wild ferment of happenings and light shows and underground films there will not emerge a new and vital art form? Who can say, as Mr. Stillman does, that we have no giants to equal Planck and Einstein and Freud? The biological sciences today are in just such a state of bursting discovery as the physical sciences were half a century ago. Where, indeed, are the Plancks and Einsteins of biology? In their laboratories, perhaps, stirring up some primordial soup in hopes of creating life from amino acids, or fiddling with chromosomes in hopes of altering human heredity. Before they get through they may make a genius out of every new baby.   J.J.T.

HORIZON is published every three months by American Heritage Publishing Co., Inc. Editorial and executive offices: 551 Fifth Avenue, New York, N.Y. 10017. Treasurer: George W. Breitkreuz. Secretary: John C. Taylor III. All correspondence about subscriptions should be addressed to: HORIZON Subscription Office, 379 West Center St., Marion, Ohio 43302.

Single Copies: $5.00; Subscriptions: $16.00 per year in the U.S. & Canada; elsewhere, $17.00

Annual indexes for Volumes I–IX are available at $1 each. A cumulative index for Volumes I–V is available at $3. HORIZON is also indexed in the *Readers Guide to Periodical Literature*. The editors welcome contributions but can assume no responsibility for unsolicited material. Title registered U.S. Patent Office. Second class postage paid at New York, N.Y., and at additional mailing offices.

COVER: This odd assemblage of fruit shapes, stone "rivets," and broken tiling is not a contemporary sculpture, but the finial of one of four spires built forty years ago by Antonio Gaudí for his Sagrada Familia church in Barcelona. HORIZON obtained this view from an enterprising local photographer, Alfredo Zerkowitz Singer, who after limbering up for a few days in the Pyrenees arrived at the church with camera, ropes, and climbing crew, and scaled a neighboring spire to *its* finial—some four hundred and twenty feet above the ground. Some other striking photographs of some of Gaudí's controversial architecture accompany an article that begins on page 28.

Before the Fall

How decadent are we?
What, really, is a "sick" society?
Are we Rome in decline? How worried should we be?
Read on at your peril

Then came the age of the Fifth Men—would that I were not one of them, but had died before or been born after! For now is a race of iron and never by day shall we have rest from labor and anguish; the Gods shall fill us with cares. . . . The father is no longer kind to his children, nor the children to the father, nor the guest true to the host that shelters him, nor friend to friend . . . Parents shall grow old quickly and be despised, and will turn on their children with a noise of bitter words . . . There shall be no more joy.   —Hesiod, *Works and Days*

Men have no doubt been bemoaning the decadence of the times since the expulsion from the Garden. But what constitutes decadence—and whether we in our time are suffering its effects —is not so easy to say. When, in the wake of civil disorder, war, and political assassination, savants declare, and our own President denies, that we are in the throes of a fatal disease, the proposition is worth exploring.

How should we explore it? Our guide is history, for "the living," as Lord Acton put it, "do not give up

The columns of a splendid temple tumble to the ground—apt symbol for the fall of proud civilizations—in this detail from François de Nome's King Asa of Judah Destroying the Idols, *done about 1625.*

their secrets with the candor of the dead." But even history is not a fixed and certain story so much as a record of dimly apprehended events onto which we project our own preconceptions, hopes, and anxieties.

What is a "sick" society? There is no better example of the difficulty of framing an answer than to begin by examining the fall of Rome—that often cited "parallel" to our own day.

According to Edward Gibbon, the fall of Rome was "the greatest, perhaps, and the most awful scene in the history of mankind." But if, as our grandmothers have repeatedly assured us, Rome was not built in a day, neither did it die in a day—lurid modern imaginations aside. The wages of sin may be death; but in the case of Rome the penalty was curiously delayed.

From 753 B.C., the traditional date of Romulus's founding of the city on the banks of the Tiber, to the death of Marcus Aurelius, that last "good emperor," in 180 A.D.—a date that may be fairly taken as marking the onset of the winter season of the empire—is a span of 933 years. But from Marcus's death in camp on the Danube, while keeping watch on the German barbarians who sought to break through the Limes and sack the empire, to the ultimate

fall of East Rome, or Constantinople, in 1453 A.D. is a span of *nearly thirteen hundred* years.

In its battle to survive, Rome bled and rallied, bled and rallied, to outlast a good many of the self-confident barbarian peoples who battered at its gates. And in that battle, too, it won something else—the nearly universal regard of mankind as the barbarian nations themselves came to aspire to nothing better than to enter into the dying empire's inheritance.

According to the early church father Orosius, the barbarian chieftain Atawulf, successor to Alaric, sacker of Rome, "had started life with an eager craving to wipe out all memory of the name of Rome . . . In time, however, experience had convinced him that on the one hand the Goths were utterly disqualified by their uncontrolled barbarity for a life under the rule of Law, while on the other hand it would be a crime to banish the rule of Law from the life of the State . . . When Atawulf divined this truth, he had made up his mind that he would at any rate make a bid for the glory that was within his reach . . . of using the vitality of the Goths for the restoration of the Roman name to all . . . its ancient greatness."

This political fantasy would not die.

By EDMUND STILLMAN

The memory of Rome haunted the Middle Ages as petty princelings aspired to re-create the grandeur of the Roman conception of law and empire. And when in the Renaissance springtime of Europe—an age that rediscovered the inner spirit of the pagan world —men looked back to Rome, it was to note, as Michel Eyquem de Montaigne put it, that "even her ruin is glorious with renown and swollen with glory."

For there was a gallantry, a quality of skeptical courage, about the empire's dying that was signally absent in Rome's ugly, pushing, parvenu years. In those early years of republican growth Rome had callously destroyed the power of such civilized contemporaries as Carthage, Macedonia, the federated Greece of the Aetolian and Achaean leagues, and Ptolemaic Egypt; had drained the wealth of the Mediterranean; dragooned whole armies of luckless Eastern *fellahin* to till its lands as slaves; pauperized and brutalized its own domestic proletariat; and ground down the individuality of all it conquered, building in place of a vigorous and diverse late classical culture a vulgar monoculture that stretched in its deadly know-nothing sameness from the Straits of Gibraltar in the west to the Caspian Sea in the east, and from the Libyan desert in the south to distant Britain.

It was only at the end of its life span—as the wealth of the empire shrank, as the cities were depopulated, as the defeats came crowding and the Roman people, once lords of the earth, were reduced to penury and anxiety— that the other Rome emerged. This was the Rome of the ideal of universal order. This was the Rome that played midwife to the Church and to the world—not the young and vulgar Rome of excess and triumph. It was the young Rome of power that was profligate—or to reverse the proposition, it was the Rome of profligacy and cruelty that was supreme in its time.

I make the point, not to deny the superior vigor of early Rome, but to stress, with all due recognition of the intellectual exhaustion and intrigue-ridden politics, the moral—or, if you like, the *spiritual*—superiority of later Rome. And I make the point, too, to stress that Rome is not really contemporary America. Whatever it is that we are witnessing in the modern world —long-haired boys and short-haired girls, sexy movies, Black Power, arson in the ghetto, semilegal pot, love-ins, draft-card burners, and militant students assaulting the office of the university president on Morningside Heights—it is *not* the Decline and Fall of the Roman Empire.

It is hard to read in Lyndon B. Johnson the Stoic lineaments of a later Roman emperor like Marcus Aurelius. General Abrams in Vietnam is not a tired and protoexistentialist Claudius Gothicus, desperately and against overwhelming odds guarding the imperial frontier. Nor is it really much easier to see the hippies, those self-proclaimed apostles of gentleness whose way of life already shows signs of passing over into a cult of anarchic violence, as the spiritual successors to the martyrs of the cross who allowed themselves, all unprotesting, to be maimed, burned, and torn apart in the arena to give witness to the Word.

To see America playing the role of a new Rome to Europe's Greece, to forecast, as does the French historian Amaury de Riencourt, the age of the "coming Caesars," to talk of the *Pax Americana,* is a new commonplace. But if all this is so—if, for example, there *is* an eerie parallel between the deaths of the Gracchi brothers, those "tribunes of the poor," and the two murdered Kennedys—are we still not a Rome *manqué?*

There is much talk in America of the responsibility of power, but it is hard to see evidence of the kind of brutal self-confidence that could sustain Rome against the terrible reverses of the Hannibalic War. One may doubt, on the evidence of Vietnam, that Americans would support a distant colonial war that proved inconclusive year after year, such as that against Mithradates, king of Pontus, who had incited the whole East to rise in guerrilla rebellion against Rome.

Is there really, in any case, a *Pax Americana?* Or is it merely that Europe is too exhausted by half a century of total wars to carry on its former role of world policeman? Would Americans really *impose* a universal peace, bloody as that task might prove? We do not seem to have the austere Roman military virtues—but we do not seem to have the vices, either.

Certainly no self-respecting Roman libertine of the noontime years would have endured the moralizing twaddle that goes along with an East Village group grope, nor would the reader of Petronius's *Satyricon* have found much to titillate his jaded senses in *Myra Breckinridge* or *Candy:* apparently dirty books and imperial vigor are not interconnected.

Sex would hardly seem to be the point. The greatest womanizer in the White House could never compare with the second of Rome's emperors, Tiberius, who, as the gossipy Suetonius informs us, "on retiring to Capri . . . made himself a private sporting-house, where sexual extravagances were practiced for his secret pleasure. Bevies of girls and young men, whom he had collected from all over the Empire as adepts in unnatural practices, and known as *spintriae*, would perform before him in groups of three, to excite his waning passions. . . . He furthermore devised little nooks of lechery in the woods and glades of the island, and had boys and girls dressed up as Pans and nymphs posted in front of caverns or grottoes; so that the island was now openly and generally called 'Caprineum,' because of his goatish antics."

Sexual profligacy, the breakdown of marriage, the transformation of the Roman peasantry from a self-respecting yeoman militia into a vicious urban mob, the hideous cruelty of a state machine that could butcher many thousands of Christians for refusing to proclaim the emperor a god—all these signs of social "degeneracy" seem quite irrelevant to the power and ultimate stability of the Roman state.

The trouble with the popular notion of the Decline and Fall of the Roman Empire is that, at bottom, it has no basis in fact. In our distorted view centuries are compressed into decades; the eras are transposed—profligacy being assumed to flourish at the end, while stoic virtues are believed to characterize the years of power. The reverse is true. As the celebrated *gravitas*—weightiness, seriousness—of the republican character deteriorated, the empire increased in size. Macedon was crushed in 197 B.C., the Seleucid Empire in 192, and Carthage in 146. Macedonia was annexed as a province in 148, and Greece itself was annexed in 146. Thus the enervating effects of fun and games! Perhaps too many weepy gospel movies in the style of D. W. Griffith and Cecil B. de Mille have warped our imaginations. For profligate Rome endured and endured, and the easy moralizer will find none of the stuff of sermons in its story. Why Rome fell in the end is something else again.

For one thing, despite the majestic ruins of roads, amphitheatres, and aqueducts that brood over the landscape of the vanished empire, Roman technology was essentially unprogressive. Rome added little to the store of inventions of the classical world. In uniting all the states of the late Hellenistic age that ringed the Mediterranean with the backlands of Europe and the Near East, Rome destroyed the smaller economic units that had flourished for centuries. But the Roman transportation system, despite the military roads, was incapable of surmounting the challenge of the large-scale transfer of goods from one end of the vast empire to another. By the same token, the failure to go beyond the use of slave labor and to apply technology (the steam engine, after all, was invented in Alexandria in the first century A.D.) prevented the growth of large-scale indus-

try, needed to supply a universal market. Rome's wealth came from conquest—as did imperial Spain's in a later age, when the conquistadors raped the Indies while at home industry decayed. When its external conquests ended, the Roman Empire was left to extract a meager wealth from its own population—which was too unproductive, and too ill-paid, to yield much.

Furthermore, the incessant wars that built the empire, even before the first Caesars ascended the throne, destroyed the fabric of the old peasant society: tens of thousands of Rome's best men, and the best men of its Italian allies, were drained off to fight in the east. Too often farms lay unworked, eventually to be bought up by a parvenu capitalist class, often ex-slaves: vulgar men who in Rome's aristocratic environment, just as in Victorian England, were left to dirty their hands with the trade that the upper classes eschewed. Unable to compete with the giant slave-staffed estates of Sicily and Egypt, the native peasantry of Italy took refuge in urban slums, there to live on the dole, denied any opportunity of meaningful employment by the competition of the ubiquitous slave labor and brutalized by the spectacle of the bloody circuses.

The slaves, with their outlandish customs and religions—the orgiastic cults of Isis, Cybele, and the Syrian Demeter—in turn adulterated the political consensus of the republic's most vigorous days, introducing the notion of an Oriental despotism, of the ruler as God manifest on earth. And if Gibbon is too harsh in describing Rome's fall as the "triumph of Barbarism and [Christian] Religion," nevertheless the Christians, with their otherworldly vision, must bear responsibility for sapping the strength of the old Stoic commitment to state service.

So, too, did the legions destroy the old political standards when the professional army stationed in Rome began to play at kingmaking. And when they learned that not only could the Praetorian Guard make emperors, but

that legions outside Rome could do so too, the result was a series of bloody, intermittent civil wars. In the century following Marcus Aurelius, there was scarcely an emperor whose reign was not ended by palace intrigue or a revolt of the troops that cost him his life. (Even though all of us must stand appalled at the recurrent violence in modern American life, we have not yet reached that point in the political process that Theodor Mommsen, the great classical historian, could describe as the change of government by a *de facto* "constitutional" right of revolt.)

This century of turmoil could only be brought to an end when Diocletian, who ruled from A.D. 284–305, transferred to the office of emperor all the trappings of Oriental divine monarchy and destroyed most of the residual liberties of the Roman people under the crushing conformity of a protototalitarian state—a state that fixed prices, wages, occupations, and the poor man's place of residence, in a new Pharaonic stasis destined to endure, in the east at least, for close to ten centuries.

But most of all, the economy decayed. Taxes grew burdensome; the civil service grew, but the gross national product shrank.

As trade among the disparate parts of the empire dried up, the provinces

OVERLEAF

"The Roses of Heliogabalus"

Most decadent of all the Roman emperors, in Gibbon's judgment, was Elagabalus (or Heliogabalus) who fell heir to the throne in A.D. 218. A priest of the Syrian sun-god, whose name he took for himself, Elagabalus dressed in flowing robes, painted his cheeks red, and took a centurion for a "wife."

What fired the imagination of Sir Laurence Alma-Tadema, the late Victorian English painter, was the legend that Elagabalus once staged an orgy in which the participants were smothered to death in a cascade of rose petals. His painting depicts a bevy of voluptuaries, all quite decorously garbed, floundering in the petals while the emperor toasts their impending fate.

The Roses of Heliogabalus *by Sir Laurence Alma-Tadema*

became increasingly autarkic, losing in the process the habit of political co-operation. The empire split into an eastern and a western half, joined only formally; and soon even these units became further fragmented. Within the provinces the same process reduced the great landed estates to a still narrower self-sufficiency, so that the unity of the provincial administration began to break up into a petty feudalism.

As the late Gordon Childe, one of the most distinguished archaeologists of our day, put it: "The bankruptcy of the Roman economy was nakedly exposed. It was proclaimed to the biologist by the decline in fertility that is notorious in all classes of the population of the later Empire. Economically, as well as scientifically, classical civilization was dead a hundred and fifty years before barbarian invaders from Germany finally disrupted the political unity of the Empire and formally initiated the Dark Age in Europe."

But in the east, where town culture and the arts of civilization had deeper roots, the fall of West Rome did not mean the end. East Rome would fight on. If we dismiss the history of later Byzantium as a mere caricature of Rome, we will still be forced to admit that great Roman soldiers and statesmen were born in the east at least until the eighth century—men like the emperor Justinian, who systematized and codified Roman law, like his generals, Belisarius and Narses, who rewon Italy from the Goths, and finally, like the tragic emperor Heraclius, who destroyed East Rome's deadly enemy, the revived Persian empire of the Sassanids, only to see half his empire fall to the first fierce onslaught of Islam.

We might end Rome's story with Heraclius, but nonetheless the period from the death of Marcus Aurelius to the final failure of Heraclius's stand against the Mohammedan hordes spans nearly five hundred years.

No, America is not Rome—it is neither so vicious nor, probably, so great. In any case, since economic decay un-derlay much of the story of Rome's ruin, we need to note that modern America remains productive and, in industrial matters, at least, innovative; even if we grant that America's imperial commitments today are over-extended, or that the dollar shudders under the dual strain of the Vietnam war and inflation at home, the ultimate economic decline and fall would seem far, far away. And Europe—in its new-found prosperity since World War II, and in its recent political self-assertion against post-1945 American predominance—is no docile Greece, no effete and passive continent resigned to its fate.

So we are not, it would seem, at the end of the story—neither America's story nor the story of the larger Western world.

Well, then, can we all roll over in our sleep? Is it all a bad dream—this presentiment of decline and fall? Alas, I suspect not. While the fall may be distant, the decline may well be upon us, and far advanced at that. In this case, we are all like the superannuated young man who, in V. S. Pritchett's phrase, had a brilliant future behind him.

The crisis transcends America. There is a nearly universal conviction abroad in the world that something is radically wrong. And this conviction does not stem from the familiar, indeed chronic, distaste voiced by the old for the ways of the young: it is far more than an angry belief that things were better done in our forefathers' day, that the young are going to hell in a handbasket. The young join with us in this subliminal conviction that something has gone unaccountably awry, and they are more than troubled—they are bitter. It is not merely that they are revolutionary: if they were that—visionary, seeking—it could be a sign of social vigor, of growth. But nowhere in our Western world today is there a revolutionary who could say, as did the youthful William Wordsworth greeting the French Revolution, that "all the world was young, and to be young was very heaven."

The new mood is dark—and it brings to mind an astute dictum of Oswald Spengler's: "Only the sick man feels his limbs."

There is a sense of possibilities foreclosed, of problems too big, of a failure of nerve of a whole society. But perhaps it is not so much a matter of diminishing *élan* as of age. The world is not new any more; modern men carry a vast weight of self-conscious history on their backs. Indeed, what underlies the contemporary sense of unease, the striving for forced, and false, parallels with the Rome of the winter years, is just this weary sense of *déjà vu*. We feel, even if our grasp of detail is shaky, that somehow it has all happened before and will happen again. Thus the search for the *pattern* of history in our day. And it is here that a man like Giovanni Battista Vico—shabby pedant, starveling professor of rhetoric at the University of Naples in the first quarter of the eighteenth century, author of *Principi di una Scienza Nuova*, the *New Science*, and grand architect of a theory of cyclical history—has something to say.

Observing the history of bygone peoples and civilizations, Vico divided the course of history into three phases—the Age of the Gods, the Age of Heroes, and the Age of Men—the last ending with a relapse into the savagery from which men initially emerged and are to emerge again and again.

Mankind, said Vico, in the centuries after Adam's fall and the expulsion from the Garden, grew wild. Max Harold Fisch, a distinguished analyst of Vico's thought, summarizes: "During the two centuries Vico allowed for this process of bestialization, the earth slowly dried, until the first thunderclaps caused by its exhalations startled these brutish men here and there in the act of shameless canine copulation with captured women, and terrified them into the shelter and secrecy of caves for their intercourse. Out of these retreats of fear and shame the first families arose, with a settled life apart in the caves of the earth, sanctioned by 'the frightful religions' started in their minds by the thunderbolts of the sky god. With settled habitations came clearing and tilling of the soil, ownership, property, morality, and burial of the dead." In this stage the father was priest and king, absolute ruler over family and those starving waifs of the forest who took refuge with the settlers; these dependents became, in time, the first slaves and serfs. So the first age—the Age of the Gods.

To repress the aspirations of the slaves, the priest-king-fathers banded together to form a stern oligarchic state—for the king of that state was merely one of the fathers, governing with their consent and expressing their common will. So the second stage— the Age of Heroes—modeled on early Greece and Rome.

But in time the slaves would develop a class consciousness and press for an ever greater share of the fruits of their labors—and, more significantly, for legal rights, for a voice in the life of the state. As they mounted their attack, gradually broadening their demands, they transformed the society; what had been a patrician oligarchy passed by degrees into a popular republic. So the last of the three ages— the Age of Men.

But the Age of Men would run its course as well. The stern virtues of the old patrician class, the virtues of a Cato, would soften in time to a complacency, an easy humanity, a taste for self-indulgence. The old religion would die—to be replaced by skeptical philosophies or cults emptied of the old fear of the gods and sustained by nothing more than a respect for decorum. The laws themselves would grow humane, liberties would grow —but the citizens would turn away from duty to the very state that succored them.

Democracy, says Vico, might well be supplanted in time by vast bureau-cratic monarchies, in the way that Ptolemaic Egypt or the Seleucid Empire superseded the old civic life of the Greeks, or imperial Rome superseded the sterner republic. Yet even these monarchies might prove more protective of the welfare of the citizen than ever he had been of himself in republican days. This process of social decline would continue until internal collapse or conquest by a better people would begin the cycle anew.

As Vico put it: "The nature of peoples is first crude, then severe, then benign, then delicate, finally dissolute" —though he had in mind no mere notion of sexual degeneracy being "dissolute." In a convenient ideology for conservatism, the very humanity of the state—of the Welfare State—was a clinical sign of an incipient decline. This delicacy of thought and mood, together with the alienation from the public life of the old order, Vico saw as "the disease of the cities." The city culture, according to Vico, was a sure sign of a civilization's advanced age.

For Oswald Spengler, an embittered product of the years following Germany's catastrophic defeat in World War I, a dark prophet of *Der Untergang des Abendlandes*, the Decline of the West (or, more accurately, the setting—the imagery is ultimately solar) is more than a sign of civilization's advancing age. It is a sign of mongrelization, of the domination of rootless men devoid of style and destiny. This is polemic, but Spengler the self-educated eccentric is more than a mere polemecist motivated by the spectacle of the collapse of the Prussian Idea under the blows of the "money civilization" of the West. His total system is far more complex.

Each society, according to Spengler, is an organism whose fate is inexorably ruled by Destiny—and this destiny is as fixed as the stars. All societies experience the four seasons: springtime, or birth; summer, or the years of high achievement; and ultimately autumn and winter—the last a time of petrifaction and eventual death.

A society in *growth* is a *Culture;* a society in *decline* is inevitably transformed from Culture into *Civilization*. Bruce Mazlish has written of the latter phase of a society's life in *The Riddle of History:* "Intellectually, it is marked by a fact philosophy as against metaphysical speculation and by a completely eclectic art and literature. Economically, it is dominated by money, and politically, by imperialism—that is, by energy directed outward under the control of a Caesar. The basic core of civilization, however, is the world city . . . Within this world-city"—how like Vico—"there is a new sort of nomad, a parasitical city dweller, rootless, traditionless, without a past. The city population is a mass, not a people or race. It is futureless. At the end, there is depopulation, the city crumbles."

Spengler's style is extraordinarily opaque. But in his own words: "If the Early period is characterized by the birth of the City out of the country, and the Late by the battle between city and country, the period of Civilization is that of the victory of city over country, whereby it frees itself from the grip of the ground, but to its own ultimate ruin. [It is] . . . dead to the cosmic, irrevocably committed to stone and intellectualism."

In the spring and high summer of a Culture the style and institutions that characterize it are *easy*—"Culture," as Spengler says, "is the self-evident." It is that which, in the growth phase, is natural for men, what is simply *done*, without thought, without striving for effect, without self-conscious display. Only when the Culture passes out of its growth phase do men begin to become aware of themselves, of what their culture has been, or means: "the sick man feels his limbs." The onset of such self-examination is a sign that the growth phase is pretty well ended —though, to be sure, this does not mean that all forms of creativity die simultaneously. The Culture, in Spengler's system, is an organic concept,

Are these the signs of decadence?

We offer here a gallery of items that are often regarded as signs of the coming Decline and Fall. But are they? Our author would probably reject many of them on the grounds that there is no historical correlation between sexual license and the end of civilization. But to him and other students of history, some of them would seem ominous. And to Oswald Spengler our very uncertainty would be a symptom of decay.

Faddist art: Mrs. Robert Scull and plaster cast

Lindner's dehumanized forms, detail

The mannish woman

The game of violence

Randomness glorified: a "happening"

Nudity flaunted, off Broadway

Juveniles exploited

Alien creeds: Mia Farrow with her guru

Alien garb: the Nehru jacket

"Anyone who is against me will look like a rat—unless I run off with Eddie Fisher.."

Gleeful tastelessness

Crime glorified: Bonnie Parker

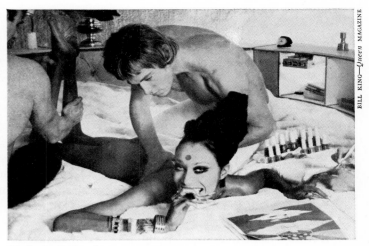

Flesh glorified: a beauty treatment

Cult of squalor: the hippie cellar where Linda Fitzpatrick was murdered

Tumorous government: a bureaucratic fortress fit for Diocletian

37 Who Saw Murder Didn't Call the Police

pathy at Stabbing of Queens Woman Shocks Inspector

By MARTIN GANSBERG

For more than half an hour respectable, law-abiding citizens in Queens watched a killer alk and stab a woman in three parate attacks in Kew ardens.

Twice the sound of their voices d the sudden glow of their droom lights interrupted him d frightened him off. Each e he returned, sought her ' stabbed her.

eath of fellow feeling in the big cities

Class war: Chicago's burned-out ghetto

not a mechanical one—and no doubt he would allow for the dying tree's sending out a tendril or two.

"When men construct an unmetaphysical religion in opposition to [inherited] cults and dogmas . . . when in art, styles are invented in place of *the* [once canonical] style that can no longer be borne or mastered; when men conceive of the State as an 'order of society' which . . . must be altered —then it is evident that something has definitely broken down."

And this fate, according to Spengler, is already upon us. We can recognize it as the coming of nihilism. Spengler is not interested in detail so much as in the *feel* of an age. Showy achievements in space, say, or in nuclear technology—the achievements, he would have argued, of a derivative technology that merely elaborates discoveries of an earlier growth phase of our civilization—will not shake his gloom. "It is easy but useless to point to the bigness of . . . modern European achievement. . . . Not external life and conduct, not institutions and customs, but deepest and last things are in question here—the inward finishedness of megalopolitan man . . . For the Classical world this condition sets in with the Roman age; for us it will set in from about the year 2000." Again we are in Rome, but it is the Rome of imperium and outward growth even if it is also the Rome of inner sterility.

To the Englishman Arnold Toynbee, the latest of this triad of philosophers of the growth and death of civilizations, technological display is even less germane; and his total message is less dark. The breakdown of a society is not an inner necessity—the consequence of some darkly apprehended, if indefinable, universal law. According to *A Study of History*, his twelve-volume masterwork, breakdown occurs when a society fails to respond successfully to challenge: in Toynbee's system the "creative minority" that leads the civilization in its growth phase suffers a failure of crea-

tivity and self-confidence.

The society, homogeneous in its earlier phases, splits into a "dominant minority" that no longer leads by exerting a magnetic charm over the mass but rules by regimentation and repression. The mass divides itself as well. An "internal proletariat," composed of all those whom the civilization has incorporated in its growth phase but who are, in his phrase, "in but not of" the society, "secede" from their previous allegiances. (The militant Negro would belong to such an internal proletariat.) Meanwhile an "external proletariat" develops on the geographical fringes. It is composed of barbarians, or in some cases civilized men of other cultures who in an earlier period aspired to incorporate themselves into the growing civilization, but who now, like Orosius's Goth, seek to destroy it or usurp its powers. (Who these proletarians are, in the case of Western civilization, is not difficult to guess. If, as the Roman satirist Juvenal said of the urban mob in the second century A.D., "the Nile and Orontes have been set flowing into the Tiber," in our age, so Toynbee asserts, the Niger has been set flowing into the Hudson. In this view men like Ho Chi Minh or Jomo Kenyatta, the former Mau-Mau head, who in the nineteenth-century noon years would have aspired to nothing more than passing as cultivated Europeans or Americans, but who now have moved to antipathy and war, are the leaders of our external proletariat.)

Toynbee, in any case, sees the process of decline as a lengthy affair. The society breaks down to enter a period of intermittent fratricidal wars; this is the "Time of Troubles." Though the life span of a society is not fixed, and though the years of decline may be interrupted by seemingly successful rallies, once the breakdown occurs and the society is splintered, nothing can save it. As the fragmentation increases, the dominant minority will attempt to pacify the society by erecting what Toynbee calls a universal state—an

empire on the model of Rome that secures a dubious peace at the cost of repression, standardization, and, ultimately, the death of all creative thought.

True creativity in these twilight years is reserved for the proletariat. The inner proletariat, according to Toynbee, creates a new religious vision—a religion that will be the mother womb of the new civilization to come. The creativity of the external proletariat is characteristically expressed in an epic poetry—as the Homeric epics were the creation of the Mycenaean war-bands who destroyed the moribund Minoan empire sometime around 1100 B.C. or the *Niebelungenlied* was the work of the Germanic tribes who battered at the frontiers of dying Rome in the fifth century A.D.

A sure sign of incipient decline is not merely the drying up of creativity but the tendency of the ruling elite to adopt the habits of thought, dress, diversion, and religion of the internal and external proletariat—those whom the society in its growth phase attracted rather than repressed, intimidated rather than imitated—so that, as in late republican Rome, the great senatorial families found themselves practicing the vices of their slaves and worshiping their gods as well.

And this is truly an ominous parallel for our day, when, whatever the moral judgment may be, our elite are engaged in a self-conscious eclecticism of arts and values, adopting the proletarian entertainments of the downtrodden poor; when the young enviously imitate the fancied life style of the submerged Negro minority, pretending, in short, as beats and hippies to be, in Norman Mailer's phrase, "white Negroes."

Even the religious imitation is present, as the old, official religion, Catholic or Protestant or Jewish, is emptied of meaning and replaced by a new search for alternative visions, those of Zen and Indian mysticism, garbled but of ultimately alien origin. In this view

—and Toynbee's, be it noted, is an eminently conservative, even reactionary, imagination—*yé-yé* styles, the proletarian vitality of the Beatles, two titanic wars in this century, and our eclectic liking for the arts of Black Africa or pre-Columbian Mexico or for Pop Art rather than the painting of Botticelli: all bespeak a breakdown of our civilization. They do so not because, the wars aside, such phenomena are intrinsically evil but because they bespeak a loss of the self-sufficiency and self-confidence of the elite —a loss of the easy appreciation and practice of the ancestral *style* that is reminiscent of Spengler's own criterion of decline.

Toynbee, like Spengler, leaves us in no doubt about where he thinks we stand, even though he coyly retires, again and again, into a tangle of verbal religiosity: ". . . a tottering civilization which has shamefully succumbed to the intoxication of a showy victory over Physical Nature, and has applied the spoils to laying up treasure for itself without being rich toward God, may be reprieved from the sentence— which it has passed on itself—of treading out the tragic path of *koros-hubris-ate;* or to translate this Hellenistic language into a Christian imagery, an apostate Western Christiandom may be given grace to be born again as the *Republica Christiana . . .*" Cynically, one may doubt that it will.

Are we dying? One may doubt that we have yet reached that point of dissolution where, in Vico's phrase, men "finally go mad and waste their substance." One may doubt the ultimately astrological intuitions of a Spengler: civilizations are not ruled by the stars. One may doubt, too, Toynbee's ultimately theological prose poem of civilizations, a gigantic Pilgrim's Progress that suffocates us with its petty pieties.

But something is there.

Our public and private characters, as Vico would put it, are certainly no longer severe. It seems fair to say that we are far advanced in an Age of Men as "discipline, respect for law, and social solidarity . . . [give] way to a humane and easy tolerance," as "philosophy [takes] the place of religion," as our characters grow "benign" and possibly even "delicate." Spengler's assertion that we are in the process of exhausting the feeling-forms and thought-forms of our civilization—which is itself a mere postscript to the great creative phase of Culture—has an uneasy ring of truth.

Have we not, just possibly, passed from culture to routine civilization? A half-century ago, when Spengler made his charge, it may have seemed the caviling of an embittered crank. There were giants in the earth in those days—men like Freud and Einstein and Kafka and Joyce and Gide and Matisse and Braque and Rilke and Gorky and Babel and Mahler and Bartók and Ives and Bergson and Croce and on and on and on . . .

But the intuition may have been right, after all. The giants have pretty much departed the scene. Is Saul Bellow really a Proust—or even a Fitzgerald? Is Marshal McLuhan really an I. A. Richards or a Wittgenstein? Is not our vaunted technology for the most part a working out in practical detail of basic theories and perceptions that are by now nearly half a century old? In what sense is the Apollo program a fundamental breakthrough comparable to Max Planck's quantum theory? And even if we reply that the biological sciences— witness DNA—are on the eve of great things, the test-tube creation of life itself, is technological expertise a true index of a society's growth or inner health? Technology is cumulative and has gone on growing throughout history independent of the rise and fall of great civilizations. Contrary to the popular view, in technological terms the Dark Ages were not necessarily a reversion. The technology of Europe *after* Rome was more advanced than it was in Rome's great days.

Even if Toynbee is a post-Victorian fuddy-duddy, can we really believe that it is a sign of social health that our elite, who once elaborated *the* style, should so blatantly imitate the vulgarities, and not the virtues, of those they once claimed to lead?

If the exploitation of the proletariat is a great crime in history, if the elite were too often oppressive or merely smug, does that mean there shall be no excellence? Shall there be no aspirations to belong to a deserving elite? Or, as in Vico's somber vision, must democracy in politics lead to a deadly statism that overlays a formless egalitarianism of the senses?

Neither Vico, nor Spengler, nor Toynbee would claim that history must repeat itself in minute detail. Rome in its twilight attained a certain majesty, but not all the civilizations of the past died as well. Others with an unkillable will to survive, like China and Pharaonic Egypt, refused to give way and went on ceaselessly, century after century, tirelessly dotting the *i*'s and crossing the *t*'s of an increasingly empty existence. Perhaps we will drag on, too—technologically capable of keeping the barbarians at bay but of little else.

When the pulse of the life of the state grows feebler, when men's imaginations grow dull, then eventually it is a good thing that, as in Rome's case, Vico's "better nation" finally comes to conquer. The arts atrophy, factions and civil wars hold sway. "In this way," says Vico, "through long centuries of barbarism, rust will consume the misbegotten subtleties of malicious wits, that have turned them into beasts made more inhuman by the barbarism of reflection than the first men had been made by the barbarism of sense."

Edmund Stillman is on the faculty of the School of Advanced International Studies at The Johns Hopkins University. Otherwise he lives, writes, and raises horses in Connecticut. Presumably he is now preparing for the Fall.

SIR ISAAC NEWTON

"Newton is, beyond dispute, the greatest scientist who ever lived,
the only one of whom it can be said:
had he not lived, the course of science might have been radically altered"

He voyaged, wrote Wordsworth, "through strange seas of Thought, alone." Such, to the poet, was "Newton with his prism and silent face." In life the eyes of that silent face were protuberant, and often they appeared glazed, which made Newton look somewhat less than intelligent. He had the dim expression of a man whose thoughts turn inward, incessantly. This was not from love of solitude or contempt for the world, for Newton looked upon the world of men and affairs with admiration, and expressed, in moments of irritation, a corresponding dislike of "mathematical trifles." He was often irritable and almost invariably somber. It was said of him by an intimate that he only laughed "but once." The event was occasioned by someone asking him what use in life Euclid's geometry was. Whereupon Newton laughed.

The incident illustrates a profound characteristic of Newton's: he always gave the briefest possible answers to questions—even at the risk of being misunderstood. In doing so he was faithful to an austere ideal: that of mathematical elegance, the aesthetic quality that mathematicians find in the most concise of demonstrations. This formal austerity Newton elevated into a personal style and the mode of his thought. In the prime of his scientific career he compressed all of mechanics into three concise laws of motion. At

This study of Newton at sixty-eight is a detail from a portrait by Sir James Thornhill, court painter to George I. Opposite, an apple tree shades a worktable at Woolsthorpe Manor, where Newton was born in 1642. His gravitational theory came to him when an apple fell at his feet one autumn day in the garden.

the end of a long life he labored to reduce all Christian doctrine to what he took to be its minimal number of essential propositions. At all times he spoke laconically, as if an excess number of words was as inelegant as an excess number of steps in a proof. Once someone asked Newton how he had made all his discoveries, and Newton replied with perfect Newtonian concision: "By always thinking unto

the problem." The answer is indisputable. He would concentrate his awesome mental powers on a problem for days, until, as he said, "gradually the light would dawn." The light that dawned was the most monumental achievement in the entire history of science, and Newton is, beyond dispute, the greatest scientist who ever lived, the only one of whom it can be said: had he not lived, the course of science might have been radically altered.

The nature of Isaac Newton's vast achievement is easier to state than to grasp, but a singular lexical fact may suggest its magnitude. During Newton's lifetime, what we know as modern science was known to many simply as "the Newtonian Philosophy." It seemed to be his own personal doctrine, and to a remarkable extent it was. He did not himself "discover" science. No one man could have done that. Science was not some compact instrument simply waiting to be used. It was rather a complex invention that men had painstakingly to put together out of quite disparate elements. Physical science is an abstruse meld. It unites, for one thing, the abstractions of mathematics, which have no physical meaning, with concrete physical phenomena, which have no inherent mathematical form. It employs a skeptical and exacting experimental method but combines that method with the most sweeping assumptions

Newton's nearest rival, the great Dutch physicist Christian Huygens, found universal gravitation repugnant to reason.

about the mechanical nature of reality. Being empirical, it assumes that truth will emerge from the investigation of things as they are; being mathematical and mechanical, it also assumes that things as they are, are never what they seem to be. How these elements might be combined is not readily apparent, but their combination and synthesis was Newton's. If modern science and its methods can be likened to a machine, then it was Newton who assembled its parts and demonstrated its awesome power.

He was a great genius, and he was born, as Einstein once wistfully remarked, at exactly the right time.

Around 1642, the year Newton was born, science was most markedly in pieces, although four of the greatest figures in the scientific revolution had already completed their work. The monk Copernicus, who began the vast enterprise by reconstructing the heavens with the sun at the center, had been dead for a century. Francis Bacon had died in 1626, Johannes Kepler in 1630, Galileo in the very year of Newton's birth. A fifth great figure, René Descartes, had already published his *Discourse on Method* and was within two years to publish his monumental treatise on the mechanical principles of philosophy. Still, it can be

said that science did not yet exist; its methods and its goals had not yet been agreed upon. What the great pioneers shared (the long-dead Copernicus excepted) was not science but a deep disdain for the Aristotelian philosophy and an overriding desire to replace it with something better. In the parlance of the day, they were "new philosophers," united in rebellion against the "old philosophy" of Aristotle.

Within this broad unity, however, the disunity among these pioneers was sharp and deep. For example, Galileo, Kepler's peer and acquaintance, looked with utter scorn upon Kepler's most fundamental conceptions. With characteristic audacity Kepler had supposed that an invisible "moving force," emanating like spokes from the sun, drags the planets around in their orbits and that a "mutual gravitation" between the earth and its companion the moon—like moving toward like—causes the tides. This radical conception, that even the unchanging heavens require some natural force to keep them in motion, was the foundation of all of Kepler's work in astronomy, yet Galileo professed to be "astonished" that so acute a man as Kepler "has nevertheless lent his ear and given his assent to the moon's dominion over the waters, to occult properties and to such puerilities." This was not mere backbiting; Galileo's disdain flowed directly from his deepest conception of what the new philosophy must be. That philosophy, first and foremost to Galileo, had to bid a good riddance to solar emanations, occult forces, and all such quasi-magical explanations of why things are as they are. It was not, in Galileo's view, the task of philosophers to fabricate fanciful hidden causes of things. It was their object to demonstrate *how* phenomena occur and to express this "how" in the simple, precise terms of mathematics. So Galileo himself had studied falling bodies and demonstrated that, in falling, a body will cover a distance proportional to the square of the time it spends falling that distance. But *why*

bodies gravitate toward the earth's center in the first place he did not choose to say.

Descartes, arriving later, disagreed with both thinkers. That invisible forces and similar occult causes must be eliminated from philosophy was indeed one of Descartes's fundamental beliefs, as it was Galileo's. Apart from "mind," the world consists only of corporeal substance, and this matter has but one real property: extension—its size, shape, and volume. No body, for example, possesses color. It merely arouses in us, due to its particular physical structure, a certain subjective sensation that we deem its color to be. The only real differences between any two things are the differences in size, shape, arrangement, and motions of the tiny corporeal particles comprising them. Bald matter and its motion must—and will—explain everything. In this stark mechanical world of Descartes's no forces, powers, spirits, or attractions exist. If a body begins to move, that motion can have but one cause: the impact upon that body of another moving body. So, according to Descartes, bodies fall to the earth because they are pushed downward by extremely fine particles that swirl around our planet, while other vast whirlpools of these same fine particles keep the planets moving in circles. There was clearly no place for Kepler's ideas in this new universe.

Descartes also found Galileo's new science inadequate. Galileo had hoped to derive certain truths through a mathematical analysis of how particular phenomena occur. In Descartes's view, however, no certainty could come of such a piecemeal enterprise. There was, he believed, but one means to certainty. The philosopher must begin with a few indisputable axioms, which he discovers by introspection. From these axioms, he then proceeds, as far as possible, to deduce by strict logic all the other basic laws and rules of nature. Galileo had supplied no such first principles. Therefore, in Descartes's eyes, he had attempted to build a house from the roof down.

The Cartesian philosophy was lucid, comprehensive, and enormously persuasive; yet not even Descartes was taken to represent all that was valued in the new philosophy. Contemporary students of nature had also to reckon with Francis Bacon, whose new program for "the advancement of learning" was diametrically opposed in spirit to the philosophy of Descartes.

Between these two new philosophers the disparities were glaring. Descartes bade men to start with first principles and then, by deduction, to explain the phenomena of the world. Bacon bade men to begin by examining phenomena and then, by induction, to work up gradually to the most general principles. Bacon called upon men to open their eyes wide to the subtle powers of nature, and he recommended experimentation as the prime means to force nature to reveal yet more of her hidden powers. Descartes, on the other hand, asked men to shut their eyes and meditate on the "clear and distinct ideas" they found within themselves. Where Bacon and the Baconians thought that all was profoundly subtle, Descartes and the Cartesians thought all was essentially plain.

Thus there existed, in no clear interrelationships, the mathematical approach of Galileo, the mechanical philosophy of Descartes, the experimentalism of Bacon, and, more obscurely, the abstruse astronomy of Kepler. Such were the leading elements of the "new philosophy" when Newton was growing up in Lincolnshire.

The Newtons were yeoman farmers who lived for some time in a meager hamlet known as Woolsthorpe. They had only one known distinction: whereas their neighbors resided in small farmhouses and thatched cottages, the Newtons had scraped up enough money to purchase the hamlet's only stone manor house. They looked on themselves as distant kinsmen of a certain Sir John Newton, Bart., and this keen sense of rank

stayed with Newton all his life. As a child, however, he was virtually an orphan and a somewhat neglected one. His father had died some months before he was born, and his mother, upon remarrying a neighboring rector, left him for several years with his grandmother. In and around Woolsthorpe he was remembered as "always a sober, silent, thinking lad, and was never known scarce to play with the boys abroad." He amused his elders by devising ingenious instruments such as sundials and water clocks. He also collected magic tricks and formulas for compounding colored inks, which he duly recorded in a notebook. Even at that age Newton was communing chiefly with himself; whittling was one of his main occupations.

Altogether he was the kind of solitary, self-sufficient youth we would instantly describe today as "mechanically inclined." Newton was also, even as a boy, much given to laying down magisterial rules of method. "Of Drawing with ye Pen," he solemnly entitled one section of entries in his notebook, and offered the following basic rule for drawing "landskips": "If you express ye sunn make it riseing or setting behind some hill; but never express ye moon or starrs but up on necessity." Thus Isaac Newton on art, aged about sixteen. The human subjects of this kingly impulse to legislate would not materialize for a long time; outwardly Newton was humble, mild, and anxious to please.

A slight scholarly superiority to the other local farm boys saved him from his preordained fate of plowing furrows in Lincolnshire. At eighteen, thanks to his uncle's intercession with his mother, he was sent off to Trinity College, Cambridge, which was to be his home for the next thirty-five years. Humbleness followed Newton to the university. At Trinity he was a subsizar, a scholar who paid his way by doing menial chores for his fellow Trinity men.

As an undergraduate Newton was particularly interested in mathematics,

Newton's intellectual adversary René Descartes dominated the thought of the day with his new mechanical philosophy.

astronomy, and optics, but he was mainly learning what there was to learn, and he won no special honors beyond being accepted for graduate studies. Awarded his bachelor's degree in January, 1665, he probably seemed merely another future don destined to teach mathematics to an endless line of indifferent Trinity students.

This lack of distinction, however, was not due to the fact that Newton's genius was ripening slowly. His genius did not ripen. It simply burst forth. Two years after Newton completed his undergraduate studies, it could be said that of all the achievements of seventeenth-century science the better half were located, then and there, inside Newton's head—and there they stayed for some time, unknown to anybody. By the end of 1666 he had invented calculus, one of the supreme accomplishments in mathematics. He had discovered a profound truth about the nature of light and color, one of the foremost achievements of experimental investigation. He had, while espying an apple fall at Woolsthorpe, conceived the moon as a body "falling" perpetually toward the earth, like the apple, and had devised a mathematical way to express the power producing these falls. He was on the way, that is, to arriving at his theory of universal

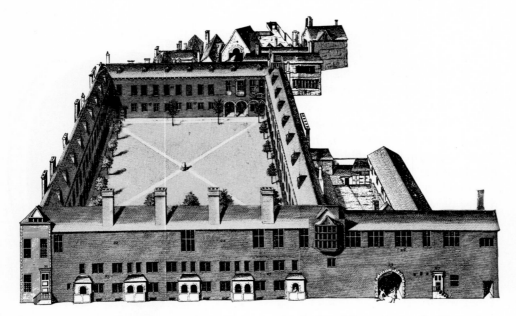

Gresham College in London, a pioneer adult education center, housed the meetings of the Royal Society until 1710.

gravitation, the greatest single discovery in physical science.

The gifts of mind Newton was bringing to bear on these topics were, of course, extraordinary, but the most extraordinary thing about them was their presence in one and the same person. The gifts were such that the possession of any one of them seems to preclude possession of the others. In the history of science the most brilliant experimental investigators have rarely been notable theoreticians; the finest theoreticians—Einstein, for example—have rarely been superior, or even adequate, experimental scientists. Yet Newton was a supreme experimental scientist and a supreme theoretical scientist as well. What is more, he alone among the very great scientists was one of the supreme figures in the realm of pure mathematics. He was to achieve in three distinct modes of thought what only a few scientists have been able to achieve in one. Such were the gifts that Newton, in his twenty-fourth year, was applying to certain comprehensive topics that took his silent fancy.

Newton's optical work—his favorite study and his first published effort—took its departure from the phenomenon of color and from the new me-

chanical philosophy of Descartes. There was nothing unusual in this. By the 1660's there was scarcely a new philosopher who was not, in some degree, a "mechanical" philosopher as well. Even professed Baconians resorted to invisible particles and the motions of these particles to explain their experimental findings. With such principles they could explain virtually anything. Given a set of facts, say those concerning air pressure, the philosopher would construct a hypothetical mechanism of invisible aerial particles endowed with hypothetical shapes and motions that seemed capable of producing the observed phenomena. Devising such mechanisms was becoming the chief business of natural philosophy; experimentation, as a result, tended to be merely illustrative. If a thinker likened air particles to little balls of wool, he could experiment with little balls of wool to show that they will expand after they are compressed—like the air.

Light, according to the leading men of science, consisted of wavelike motions in Descartes's whirling subtle matter, or ether. These waves radiated evenly from a light source, like ripples in a pond when a pebble is dropped into it. Light from the sun was pure, homogeneous, and, of course, colorless. Color, then, was the effect produced when this uniform sunlight became disturbed or modified in some mechanical way or other. Light modified in one way produced one sort of

color sensation. The same colorless light striking a body with a different sort of surface structure would be modified in a different way and so produce a different sort of color sensation. Since light when it passes through a prism will appear as a spectrum of colors on a wall, it was held that the prism, in refracting (i.e., bending) the light passing through it, also disturbed white light and so produced the spectrum. Such was the prevailing view when young Newton bought some prisms and pushed the experimental method farther than it had probably ever been pushed.

What Newton did was grasp a certain discrepant fact that he refused to explain away until it yielded the basis of an extraordinary discovery. This discrepancy arose in a precise experiment he made with a prism after many months of trial. He cut a circular hole, one-quarter inch in diameter, in the closed shutter of his room at Trinity College. Through this hole a narrow beam of sunlight entered his darkened chamber. Placing a prism near the hole, he cast the well-known spectrum of colors against the opposite wall. What he now saw, with the eye of a mathematician, others had seen but overlooked: the spectrum of colors, instead of being circular—because the hole in the shutter was circular—was an oblong. This curious elongation of the circle seized his attention.

As Newton well knew, there existed a mathematical law, discovered by Descartes, for determining how much a ray of light will be bent when it passes through a prism at any given angle. According to that law the beam, in passing through Newton's prism, ought to have cast upon the opposite wall a circle of colors $2\frac{5}{8}$ inches in diameter. The oblong image, he found, was indeed $2\frac{5}{8}$ inches *wide*, but it was $13\frac{1}{4}$ inches *high*—five times longer than it should have been. The top part of the beam had been bent more than it ought to have been according to the law of refraction; the bottom part of the beam less, which was why the beam's height was elongated. Something was radically wrong with the beautifully precise law of refraction.

Here Newton might have stopped. There was a ready means to explain away the odd elongation. Such an explanation followed, moreover, from the very nature of color itself. Newton could have said (as his adversaries eventually *did* say) that the prism, in modifying the light waves to produce colors, also spread them out somewhat to produce this elongation. It was that simple, and quite in line with mechanical principles. The explanation by "spreading," however, had one drawback; it would mean setting aside the law of refraction, and this Newton found disagreeable. Great scientists, it has been said, are perfect mixtures of credulity and skepticism. Newton, for reasons that go straight to the heart of his scientific method, chose to believe the law of refraction and to doubt the prevailing doctrine of colors.

He set aside for the moment the whole question of colors and focussed his attention solely on this apparent flaw in the regularity of refraction. Taking a second prism, he placed it between the first prism and the wall and intercepted different parts of the refracted beam. This was the "crucial experiment." In making it Newton discovered that the part of the beam that was bent too much the first time was also bent too much when refracted a second time—exactly the same amount too much. The part of the beam that was bent too little was, when refracted again, again bent too little—exactly the same amount too little. Any time a given part of the beam was refracted by the prism, it always exhibited the same fixed degree of bending, or refrangibility. Refraction, in other words, was lawful and regular for the several parts of the light beam, though not for the beam as a whole. "And so," Newton concluded, "the true cause of the length of that Image was detected to be no other, than that *Light* consists of Rays *differently refrangible,* which

. . . were, according to their degrees of refrangibility, transmitted towards divers parts of the wall."

Now it was not lost upon Newton that rays "differently refrangible" were also differently colored. When his second prism intercepted the blue part of the refracted beam, not only did that part bend to the same degree, it also remained blue. No amount of further refraction could change the color, just as no amount of further refraction could change that ray's degree of refrangibility. "To the same degree of Refrangibility," he then concluded, "ever belongs the same color, and to the same color ever belongs the same degree of Refrangibility."

As Newton now saw, something was wrong with the prevailing theory of colors. The doctrine that colors are produced when pure colorless light is disturbed could not be sustained. According to that theory, the prism causes a change in homogeneous light that results in the production of a color. A second refraction of this changed light ought, therefore, to change it more, producing yet another color. This was not the case. Blue remained blue, red stayed red. These and five other "primary colors" could not be changed no matter how many times they were refracted. The prism, therefore, did not modify pure white light, it merely *separated* different parts of white light according to their fixed and distinctive degrees of bending. So Newton concluded: "Colors are not *Qualifications* [i.e., modifications] *of Light*, derived from Refractions, or Reflections of natural Bodies (as tis generally believed), but *Original* and *connate* properties, which in divers Rays are divers. Some Rays are disposed to exhibit a red color and no other; some a yellow and no other . . ." White light, pure homogeneous light from the sun, was not, as everyone believed, pure and homogeneous at all. It was, said Newton, "a confused aggregate of Rays" endowed with different degrees of refrangibility and different dispositions to cause a

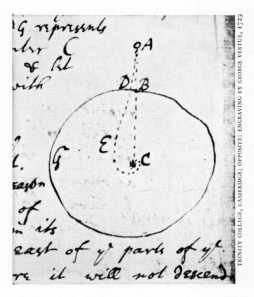

An erroneous solution of a gravity problem appeared in a 1679 letter from Newton to Robert Hooke. Irked by Hooke's blunt correction, Newton decided it was time to perfect his gravitational theory.

color sensation within us. Against all reason, so it seemed, colors were inherent in ordinary colorless light.

In an essay of thirteen mercilessly concise pages Newton set forth his discovery. Then in 1672, six years after making it, he presented it to the world of science, or rather to its illustrious new epitome, the Royal Society of London. With no false modesty whatever he described it to the membership as "the oddest if not the most considerable detection wch hath hitherto beene made in the operations of Nature." With that, Newton sat back to await acclaim. Instead, to his dismay, he found himself in the most exasperating of disputes.

The two great students of light, Robert Hooke at the Royal Society and Christian Huygens of the French Académie des Sciences, had their own theory of colors—the prevailing one. More decisively, they had their own ingrained conception of what the new mechanical philosophy was supposed to be. To them it meant devising mechanical hypotheses to explain given sets of facts. This unknown Isaac Newton, as far as they could see, had merely offered an alternative "hypothesis"—and how Newton hated the

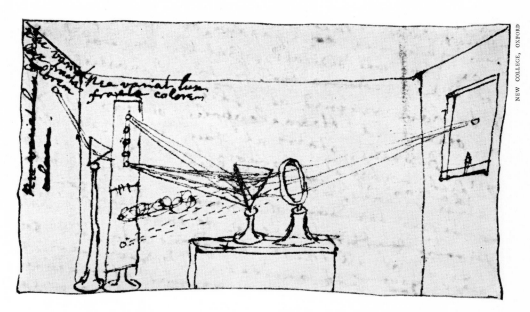

term! He had, as they saw it, explained colors by *supposing* that seven primary colors somehow pre-existed in white light, a hypothesis hard to believe. Then, to explain how a prism produces the colored spectrum, Newton, in their view, had further supposed that these differently colored rays were differently refrangible. It was, they conceded, an "ingenious" hypothesis, though distinctly inferior to their own.

With increasing vexation Newton tried to explain to his critics that they had turned his discovery upside down. He had not invented a hypothesis about color and then fitted it to the facts. The very reverse was true. He had found directly from experiment "certain properties of light . . . which if I did not know to be true, I should prefer to reject as vain and empty speculation, than acknowledge even as hypothesis." He had not supposed that white light was a confused bundle of rays differently refrangible; he was driven to that conclusion by his experimental findings. These findings could not be explained by the prevailing theory, as he pointed out to Hooke with biting scorn. His critics remained unconvinced.

For Newton it was a bitter experience. He felt cheated and victimized. He had offered the world a great new discovery, but the grandees of science had robbed him of his credit because his discovery did not square with their own mechanical preconceptions. To Newton, who had not the smallest doubt about his own immense superiority, there was only one recourse: the grandees must be taught like children what the true method of philosophy is. He told them: "First, to inquire directly into the properties of things, and establish them by experiment; and then to proceed more slowly to hy-

Simple scientific instruments of Newton's (opposite) include a prism, a mathematical dial, upper right, and a box of "Napier's bones" for calculating logarithms.

potheses for explaining them. For hypotheses should be subservient only in explaining the properties of things, but not assumed in determining them." To call an experimentally discovered property false because it contradicts a plausible hypothesis is to reverse the order of inquiry. Such was Newton's advice to his elders, and its implications are profound. Natural philosophy, he was arguing, must rid itself of the shackles of mere rationality. The properties of things, experimentally established, may *seem* unintelligible and inexplicable according to prevailing principles of reason and philosophy. Yet properties they are, and they must not be rejected a priori according to the principles of any philosophical scheme, including the one of mechanical philosophy. But Newton was only a young and obscure mathematics professor, and it would take more than a few irate letters to imprint his conception of science on the minds of men.

After this, his first public encounter with other men, Newton was bitter in the way that a haughty and capricious child is bitter. He fumed and sulked and withdrew into the thick shell of his temperament. From Cambridge he was heard to mutter peevishly that natural philosophy was "litigious" and filled with "no end of fancying." When men approached him with scientific questions, he could reply loftily that he had "laid aside philosophical speculations"; and in fact he often did. For long periods of time he preferred

This 1671–72 sketch shows the crucial experiment in which Newton's second prism, left, re-refracts the light beam.

investigating the doctrine of the Trinity (which he secretly doubted), the legal authority of the Nicene Council (which he wished to undermine), and the prophecies in the Book of Daniel (which he hoped to decipher). For Robert Hooke, who dared to criticize him before the Royal Society, he burned with barely concealed hatred. It was to Hooke, actually, that Newton addressed his famous "modest" remark that if he had seen farther, it was by standing on the shoulders of giants. He meant the remark as a pointed reminder that he did in fact see farther. Toward the illustrious society, for harboring Hooke, he pretended a polite indifference and even requested that he be stricken from the membership—on the childishly specious grounds that he could not afford the dues. The society, with utmost respect, forewent the dues, and Newton, mollified, returned the favor by presenting them in 1675 with the dazzling fruit of further inquiries into the nature of light and color. His report resulted in yet another quarrel with the irrepressible Hooke, and Newton retreated even more deeply into frigid aloofness.

Rule or sulk was the principle of Newton's life, until the day would come when he would rule like a monarch. In the meantime he led a monk-

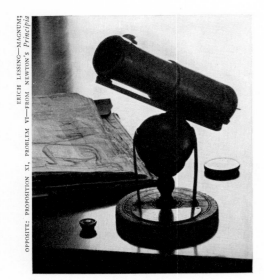

Newton's trail-blazing invention, a reflecting telescope, was built by him and presented to the Royal Society in 1671.

ish life at Cambridge as a fellow of Trinity College and Lucasian Professor of Mathematics who gave abstruse public lectures that few students attended and nobody understood. He did not have many friends at the university, which he looked on as a backwater not quite fit for a gentleman. There was little warmth in his character, and what there was seemed reserved for his widowed mother, whom he duly visited each year at Woolsthorpe.

For a man who hated to be wrong—who dreaded even appearing to be wrong—the theory of universal gravitation presented a vexatious quandary, and one that Newton lived with for a long time. Unless that theory could be proved true beyond a doubt, it would be rejected by every rational thinker as false, pernicious, and even laughable. This is the most important historical fact about the theory of gravitation. Newton's resolution of the quandary was characteristic. From the autumn day at Woolsthorpe when the idea first entered his mind until the day eighteen years later when he sat down to write about it, the notion of universal gravitation took its place alongside Newton's doubts about the Trinity in his library of secret beliefs. Then, when he published the theory, he produced the greatest single work in the history of science: the mighty *Philosophiae Naturalis Principia Mathematica*, the mathematical principles of natural philosophy.

As its prime challenge to credibility the gravity doctrine proposes that the center of a material body can, in some utterly mysterious fashion, draw, or "attract," another body across millions of miles of space without being in any way in contact with it. This inexplicable "action-at-a-distance" is further held to act instantaneously, regardless of how far apart the two bodies are. It is, moreover, a power that is miraculously inexhaustible, for it never seems to weaken. It is a power, too, that nothing whatever can balk or diminish, since it penetrates every known substance. It is everywhere and nowhere, a paradoxical principle that cannot, on the face of it, be accepted.

At the time that Newton conceived it, this principle of attraction was never less likely to be accepted, for it ran counter to everything that the new philosophy so confidently represented. By most people who thought about the matter at all, action-at-a-distance was held to be impossible. To mechanical philosophers the only conceivable cause that could operate in nature was the impact of one body upon another. Attractive powers were simply part of that vast arsenal of nonsense that the "moderns" had relegated to the ash heap: something not to be proposed, as one new philosopher remarked, "if you do not wish to be laughed at." A philosopher who was merely rational would not have entertained the idea of a universal attraction even in the privacy of his thoughts. This is not a rhetorical assertion. The fundamental discovery that points the way to universal gravitation was made independently by both Newton and Huygens. With this discovery—great in itself—Huygens did nothing, Newton everything.

The discovery is known as the law of centrifugal force. As a problem to be solved it arose from the inertia principle laid down in 1644 by Descartes: a material body, unless impeded by another body, will naturally move in a straight-line course at constant speed forever. When a body travels in a circle, therefore, it must be constantly "endeavoring" to move in its natural rectilinear course along a tangent to the circle. A body twirling on a string is pulled back by the string, but the endeavor, as Huygens observed, is felt as a "tension" on the taut string. Both Newton and Huygens found a means to express mathematically this endeavor to fly from the center of rotation. Gifted with hindsight, we see its immediate application to the heavens, where the planets, too, move in orbits. Plainly they must be endeavoring to fly from their centers of rotation. Some power, therefore, equal to this centrifugal tendency must be exerted in the opposite direction, because the planets do not, obviously, fly away. Great scientist though Huygens was, it never occurred to him to conceive of this counterpower as a pull, or attraction. Indeed, why should it have? Planets are not attached to the sun by strings, and imagining invisible strings or immaterial pulls would be puerile. Huygens supposed, as Descartes had, that ethereal whirlpools continuously *push* each planet back into its orbit, just as a whirlpool surrounding the earth causes a piece of fruit to be pushed toward the earth's center. Apples could have fallen at Huygens's feet through eternity, and he would never have supposed otherwise. Being a rational philosopher, he was a prisoner of the "true and sane philosophy" all his life. Newton was not, for he was never merely a rational philosopher.

Once again, a perfect mixture of credulity and skepticism lay behind the intuitions of genius. A conviction more powerful than the "true and sane philosophy" colored Newton's thoughts, and in doing so, liberated them. The conviction was a religious one. Consistent with his doubts about Christ's divinity, Newton believed as fervently as any Lincolnshire Puritan in the fierce, absolute God of the Old

Testament, the Hebraic God of arbitrary power and mysterious ways. Newton believed, and longed to find reason for his belief, that the providential God had not only created the world but ruled it and sustained it every moment by his will. A Supreme Being who merely created a world that ran by itself was, to Newton, the god of disguised infidels like M. Descartes, whom he detested as vehemently as any rustic clergyman. To prove that God truly governed and sustained his creation was the deepest purpose of Newton's life. This purpose and conviction gave Newton the liberty to doubt that the impact of bodies was the ultimate cause of all natural phenomena. He was willing, indeed eager, to imagine that the ultimate principle was not matter at all but immaterial powers: "active principles," he called them, directly propagated by the lawful will of God. If such immaterial powers demonstrably existed, then the world could not survive for a moment without the direct action of the Creator, and the providence of God would be upheld against the disguised infidelity of the mechanical philosophy.

So it was not inconceivable to Newton, for example, that bodies should fall toward the earth's center by means of an immaterial attractive power exerted toward the earth's center. Thus, when the famed apple fell, he was free to conceive that the very same power extended far beyond the earth's surface and caused the moon, too, to "fall" toward the earth. Never mind that such a power would make no sense to the new philosophers; it could be investigated nonetheless. Clearly this "fall," which was directed toward the earth's center, was equal to the moon's tendency to fly from that center, since the moon remained in its path. Because he now knew how to measure the centrifugal force, Newton could also calculate this balancing tendency. Specifically, he could calculate how far in any one second the moon was being pulled toward the

earth. Also he knew how far gravity would draw a falling apple in one second's time: 16.1 feet. Were the force pulling the moon and the force pulling the apple the same force? By comparing the two one-second falls Newton reached an interesting result. The power, if indeed it was the same power, grew weaker the farther away from the earth it had to act. What was more tantalizing, it grew weaker almost but not quite according to a simple mathematical rule: the gravitational force diminished in proportion to the square of the distance; at three times the distance, it was one-ninth its strength, and so forth. Almost but not quite, since Newton's first calculations were somewhat crude. This was the point he had reached as far back as 1666 at Woolsthorpe, before anybody but his professors knew his name. For thirteen more years Newton kept his gravitational work at the back of his mind, while he turned to more immediately fruitful tasks: his optics, calculus, and his diligent inquiries into esoteric branches of divinity.

The next great move came in 1679, when Newton discovered to his dismay that there was one other man entertaining the idea of a gravitational attraction varying inversely with the square of the distance. He was none other than the man Newton hated most: Robert Hooke. Gravitation was, in Hooke's hands, only a daring idea, and beyond a few close friends, including the mathematician-turned-architect Christopher Wren, nobody paid the least attention to Hooke's grandiose "hypothesis." Nobody, that is, until he flaunted it before Newton in the course of a frigidly polite exchange of letters. That a "mere smatterer in mathematics," as Newton referred to Hooke, should discourse boldly to *him* about an inverse-square law of gravity was more than Newton could bear. He sat down to prove to himself that he knew more about the matter than Hooke would ever know. Using calculus, the mighty mathe-

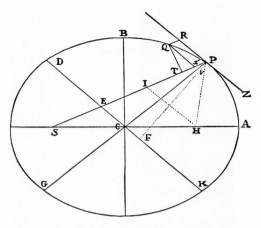

A key proof in the Principia *shows geometrically that a body, P, moving in an elliptical path is attracted to focus S (the sun) with a force varying inversely with the square of the distance SP.*

matical tool that he himself had invented (and so far kept to himself), Newton brought the gravity law one giant step closer to reality. He demonstrated mathematically that such a force, varying inversely with the square of the distance, would "bend" a moving body into an exactly elliptical orbit. This was a fundamental confirmation of the theory, for by Kepler's law the ellipse is the actual path of the planets. Since such a proof was beyond the powers of anybody, including Hooke, Newton was satisfied to drop the subject again. He had gained a private triumph, so private, indeed, that he set aside the papers containing his proofs and lost them.

Such secretiveness is more bizarre even than it might seem. Had Newton turned his back, hermit-fashion, on the world, it would have been odd but understandable. But Newton had not turned his back on the world. In 1679 he hungered as much as ever for honors and acclaim and the friendship of celebrated men. He longed to be praised, but he feared being criticized. This was the fine torture Newton's character had contrived for him: to be wretchedly suspended between fear of the world and a hunger for worldly success. So, in the dim privacy of his chambers, he often wrote long, polished essays, drafting them not once but several times, as if the very act of

Newton's quarters as a Trinity Fellow look out upon the master's lodge, where he was knighted by Queen Anne in 1705.

writing them out allayed his hunger to be read and recognized.

The forces pushing and pulling at him must have been very nearly in balance, because four years after triumphing over Hooke the mere coaxing of a tactful stranger convinced Newton to declare all that he knew about universal gravitation. The stranger, a brilliant young astronomer named Edmund Halley, simply approached Newton as he liked to be approached: as a supplicant begging help from the master. Halley now informed Newton that Hooke and Wren had been toying with the idea of a universal attraction but could explain nothing with it. If such a force existed, he asked Newton, what path would it move the planets in? "An ellipse," said Newton, remarking casually that he had proved the proposition but had mislaid the papers. The record of that famous meeting is lost, but we can imagine a thunderstruck Halley begging the strange man before him to set it all down. This Newton promptly did. In twenty months of incredibly concentrated effort Newton completed the *Principia Mathematica*. Published at Halley's expense, it appeared in the summer of 1687 and sold for seven shillings.

Simply to look at, the *Principia* is dazzling. It appears to be some kind of awesome geometry book, packed with propositions and theorems that are rigidly demonstrated by geometrical proofs accompanied by intricate diagrams. It looks, moreover, like a geometry raised to some higher power, for its subject is not static lines and areas, but "forces" that vary and "bodies" that move and accelerate; a geometry that is to the old geometry of Euclid as a motion picture is to a still photograph. Like a geometry book, too, the *Principia* is set forth in the grand deductive manner of ancient Greek mathematics. Beginning with a brief set of definitions and axioms—the three laws of motion—Newton proceeds step by step to deduce a vast array of propositions of ever-increasing complexity; some of them, indeed, deduced solely for the sake of deducing them. Having at last unburdened his mind, Newton, it seems, was determined to empty it. The relentless march of the proofs reaches its grand climax in Book Three with Newton's demonstration of the truly astounding proposition that between *any* two bodies in the universe there exists a mutual attraction that varies inversely with the square of the distance between them and directly with the product of their masses. This is the law of "universal gravitation." *Quod erat demonstrandum* Newton could justly write. Nonetheless it is certainly action-at-a-distance with a vengeance, for gravity, according to Newton, acts not only between the vast heavenly bodies but between any two particles of matter whatever. How two flecks of dust can attract each other according to Newton's law is something that no mechanism of hypothetical pushes would ever be likely to explain.

Nor does the *Principia* end here. With his law firmly established, Newton now "returns to the phenomena," as he says, in order to unravel mysteries that had baffled thinkers for millenniums. With his law he will explain mathematically why the twice-daily

tides occur and why there are spring tides and neap tides. He will even calculate how high the tide reaches in mid-ocean. He will explain, at last, the mysterious path of the comets, demonstrate that the globular earth is flattened at the poles and calculate by how much. He will estimate the mass of the sun and planets and explain why the axis of the earth makes its own revolution once every twenty-five thousand years, a problem that even Kepler had pronounced to be insoluble. He will explain the general motions of the moon and account mathematically for a variety of subtle perturbations in the moon's motions that had long puzzled astronomers. By his law of gravitation he will not only explain a vast array of phenomena, he will explain them in terms more precise than anyone had dreamed possible. From only a few laws of motion, themselves derived from phenomena, he has locked the universe into one lawful system, as comprehensive as the most daring speculations of ancient Greek philosophy and as precise in its operation as a railway timetable. The achievement was a titanic one, as readers saw at once.

Yet the fundamental problem remained: what, after all, is this impalpable attractive force that acts at a distance, against all reason, all philosophy, and all sound sense? The question haunts the pages of the *Principia*, as it must have haunted Newton himself. Time and again he anxiously warns his readers not to misunderstand him. He does *not* believe that a material body can literally "attract" another body from a distance. The attractive force of which he speaks is not a physical pull at all. He is, he explains, "considering those forces not physically, but mathematically: wherefore the reader is not to imagine that

CONTINUED ON PAGE 112

A solitary professor's long-time home, Newton's college chambers, here lighted, stood adjacent to Trinity's Great Gate.

GAUDI

The great outsider of modern architecture is back in favor. Was he simply an inspired freak, or was he the father of an organic, emotional style that is just coming into its own? Our author's conclusion: a supreme artist, but one Gaudi is enough

Do you like Gaudí? Not so long ago you could smile indulgently when you answered. Liking or disliking the bizarre buildings of Antoni Gaudí i Cornet was in about the same cocktail category as liking or disliking Tiffany glass, cast-iron lilies, and other turn-of-the-century fantasies. You could share the surrealist enthusiasm of Salvador Dali for "the terrifying, edible beauty" of forms and textures like those on the opposite page, or you could agree with the French critic Maurice Casteels, who complained that one of Gaudí's apartment houses, the Casa Milá, was "adorned with abscesses." Whatever you thought did not commit you to much, for Gaudí was presumably the great outsider of twentieth-century architecture, a provincial freak generated by the chance encounter of genius with the Gothic revival, Moorish influences, Catalan craft traditions, Art Nouveau, Spanish religiosity, and a Barcelona building boom.

Today the context for the question has changed. In recent years many visual-art consumers, aided by such taste makers as shelter magazines, paperback professors, modern museums, abstract-expressionist painters, and antique dealers, have shifted their allegiance from geometric forms to organic, from the rational to the emotional, from progressivism to historicism—in general, from classicism to romanticism. Many architects anticipated or have joined the shift: Alvar Aalto even before World War II; Le Corbusier, Frank Lloyd Wright, and Eero Saarinen, in such familiar monuments as the Ronchamp chapel, the Guggenheim Museum, and the TWA Terminal at Kennedy Airport; Philip Johnson, Edward Durell Stone, Louis I. Kahn, Paul Rudolph, and a score of lesser creators in dozens of trend-confirming works. Such terms as "Brutalism" and "neo-Liberty" (from the recent Art-Nouveau revival in Italy) have acquired international currency. Engineers have encouraged the movement by favoring structures with grid vaults that look like Brobdingnagian lace and hyperbolic paraboloid roofs that look like double-curved sea shells. Although functionalism and faith in the right angle are still much with us, their doctrinal basis has been shaken by an insistence on designs that respond to psychological as well as economic and technical requirements.

In these circumstances Gaudí has begun to seem rather more cen-

A devout Catholic, Gaudí, above, at age seventy-two, takes part in a Barcelona holy day procession in 1920.

OPPOSITE

Shark Fins on a Roof

These weird shapes, covered with a crazy quilt of broken tiles, adorn the roof of a gatehouse that Gaudí built as a part of the Park Güell, outside the city of Barcelona, between 1900 and 1914.

By ROY McMULLEN

A whiplash curve of tiled bench, top, forms the rim of a broad terrace in the Park Güell, now a municipal park. Above, a gatehouse, looking like the entrance to fairyland, guards the road into the park.

OPPOSITE

A Harlequinade of Benches

The broken-tile facing of these swirling benches, created by Gaudí in about 1908, forms patterns that appear to anticipate modern abstract painting.

tric than eccentric, in spite of his occasional air of having jumped from a lecture on medievalism straight into a Dada demonstration. It follows that merely liking or disliking him is not enough. He and his singular achievement merit evaluation, both for their own sake and for the light they may throw on what is happening now.

Evaluating the man himself is relatively easy, for he was a truly splendid amalgam of late Romantic and early modern conceptions of the architect as culture hero. He mixed John Ruskin's earnestness with a Catalan variety of William Morris's zeal, a strong belief in the sacredness of handwork, a veneration for nature, and a faith in his own powers that at times resembled the cosmic crankiness and harsh egotism of the elderly Wright. In politics he was an ardent Catalan separatist who stubbornly refused to speak the Spanish in which he had been educated, and something of a liberal: at least he was involved at one time in the co-operative movement and was interested in housing for workers. He was a brilliant theorist and a witty, mordant conversationalist who for many years frequented the literary salons of Barcelona and counted poets, painters, musicians, and philosophers among his friends. Everything he thought and did was steeped, however, in his religious sentiments, which were those of a conservative Roman Catholic and a tireless student of medieval symbolism.

Although he was handsome, and a Beau Brummell in his prosperous youth, he never married and apparently had only one brief love affair. He fortified his celibacy with long walks and a vegetable diet (plus, one can guess, the savagely erotic shapes he incorporated in many of his buildings). Around 1910, when he was fifty-eight, he gave up his career as one of the favorite architects of the affluent new Barcelona bourgeoisie and began to devote himself almost entirely to the construction of his vast church of the Holy Family, the Sagrada Familia, on which he had been working since 1884.

Eventually he became a bad-tempered hermit, dressing poorly and living in his workshop on the church grounds. When construction funds ran low, he went out on the street, hat in hand. The end was squalidly dramatic, with overtones of martyrdom. On June 7, 1926, shortly before his seventy-fourth birthday, he was struck by a streetcar near the Sagrada Familia and badly injured. He was not recognized right away, and—apparently because his old clothes marked him as a person of no importance—he was not treated immediately. He died three days later on a pauper's bed in a local hospital.

Fairly brief trips to southern France, Majorca, Morocco, and Castile were his only ventures outside his native Catalonia, and so the bulk of his production is concentrated at Barcelona. In and near the city are the following important constructions: the Casa Vicens, a town house designed in 1878, when Gaudí was twenty-six and had just been awarded the official title of architect; the unfinished Sagrada Familia; the Palacio Güell, a town house built between 1885 and 1889 for his principal patron, the textile manufacturer Eusebio Güell; the Finca (estate) Güell, of which the chief extant parts are the gatehouse and stables, under way as early as 1887; the College of Santa Teresa de Jesús, built between 1889 and 1894; the Casa Calvet, a town house finished for the most part in 1899; the Bell Esguard, a villa erected between 1900 and 1902; the Park Güell, a housing

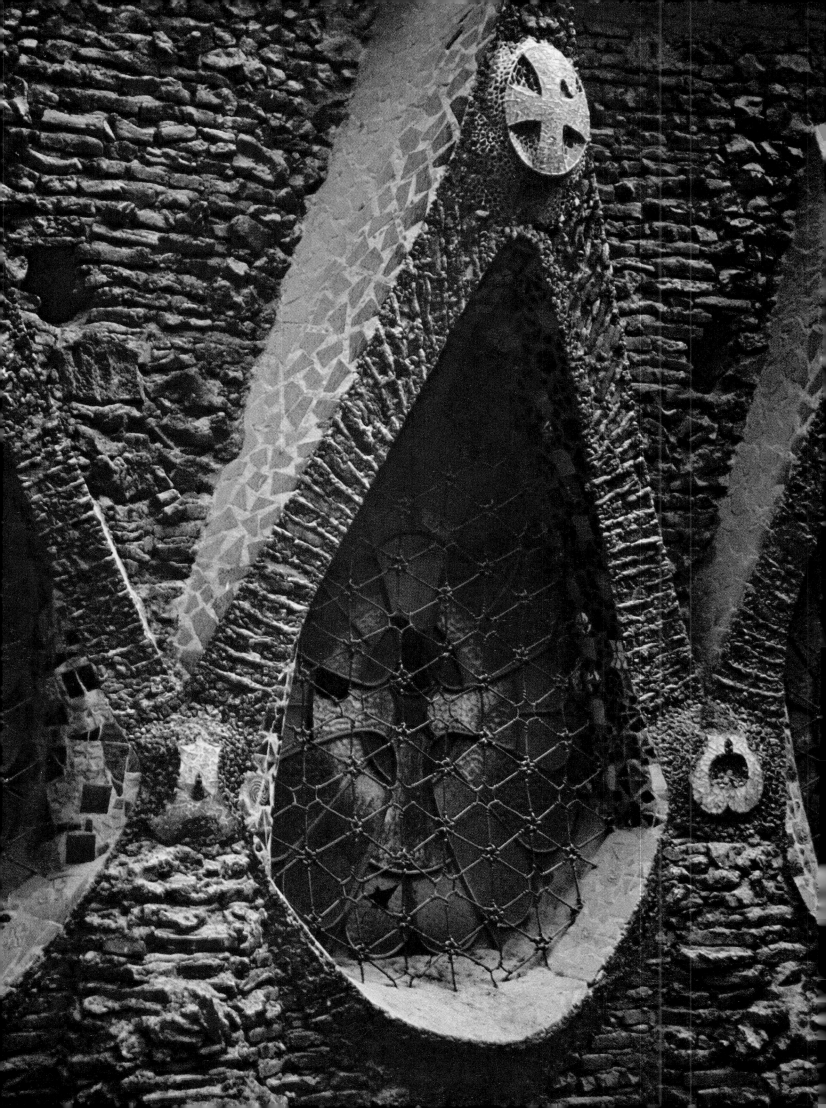

development begun in 1900, abandoned in 1914, and eventually converted into a municipal park; the Casa Batlló, an apartment house extensively remodeled by the architect between 1905 and 1907; and the already mentioned Casa Milá, begun in 1905 and left unfinished, strictly speaking, in 1910 (the whole edifice was intended to be the pedestal for a giant statue of the Virgin). A few miles west of the city, at Santa Coloma de Cervelló, there is the crypt of the Colonia Güell chapel, the only completed part of a textile workers' housing project that took Gaudí's attention intermittently from 1898 until 1915.

The spread of the dates and the number of unfinished projects are evidence of how wildly expensive these creations must have been, even at a time, and in a country, of cheap labor. Nevertheless, the sheer mass of the achievement is impressive, and it is bound to evoke a question from a sensible first-time viewer. Granted that such architecture could be imagined by some isolated visionary, how in the world did it ever come to be financed and actually built?

Part of the answer is that the Barcelona of the late nineteenth and early twentieth centuries was in some ways like the Chicago of the same period—the Chicago of such innovating architects as William Le Baron Jenney, Dankmar Adler, Louis Sullivan, D. H. Burnham, and J. W. Root. It was a brutal, anarchic city in which assassination was common and bombing or arson was likely at any moment to become epidemic; during 1907 and 1908 some two thousand bombs exploded in the streets, and in 1909 twenty-two churches and thirty-four convents were burned. It was a provincial capital struggling for power against the reactionary regime in Madrid. But it was also, like its contemporary Chicago, a growing city. In the 1860's it had demolished its medieval walls and begun to expand into the quarters that are still sometimes referred to as the Ensanche, the "enlargement." Its port, its industry, and its banking facilities, all helped considerably by the opening of the Suez Canal, were prospering. In sum, a lot of enterprising Catalans were making a lot of money rapidly, and they were ready to invest in the kind of prestige architecture that might serve to legitimate them as a new upper class.

Another part of the answer, however, is that Barcelona was in many ways not at all like Chicago, for there was no Spanish equivalent for the value system of American capitalism and not much reality to the Spanish middle class. The new men in Catalonia tended to be aristocrats making money or moneymakers hoping to become aristocrats (Gaudí's generous patron became Count Güell in 1910). And so, while Chicago was developing the skyscraper and a rational commercial architecture, Barcelona was dreaming of reviving the glory of its medieval era and—after about 1900—investing more and more heavily in Modernismo, the Catalan form of Art Nouveau. Gaudí was not alone in his addiction to expensive fantasy; indeed, several of his contemporaries in Barcelona—designers like José Puig y Cadafalch and Luis Doménech y Montaner—frequently outdid him in catering to the desire of an opulent, somewhat unreal social class for an opulent, somewhat unreal architecture—an architecture designed for amazement as much as for convenience and delight.

But Gaudí was certainly alone in his talent and in the fierce energy with which he turned the Catalan economic and social situation into

FROM *Introduccion a la Arquitectura de Gaudí* BY JUAN-EDUARDO CIRLOT. EDITORIAL RM, BARCELONA—ARCHIVO MAS, BARCELONA

FOTO ALEU, AMIGOS DE GAUDI

The porch of the chapel crypt at the Colonia Güell, top, is an evidence of Gaudí's genius for creating aberrant parabolic forms in stone and brickwork. Inside the crypt, above, the irregularly cut columns suggest the rough makeshift of an early catacomb.

OPPOSITE

Window for a Crypt

This teardrop window, set in a wall of irregular bricks and debris, admits a dim, stained light to the inside of the crypt of the chapel at Colonia Güell.

OVERLEAF

A Melting Gothic Cathedral

The unfinished church of the Sagrada Familia, looking like a medieval cathedral half melted by the sun, towers grotesquely over Barcelona. Some eighty years after work was started only this façade —the Transept of the Nativity—has been completed.

ARCHIVO MAS, BARCELONA

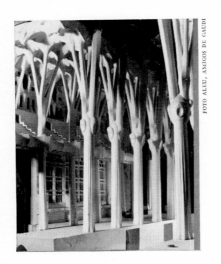

To complete the interior of the Sagrada Familia architects have made a model, top, of the nave from a few sketches of Gaudí's that survived the Spanish Civil War. A chief document, center, is his sketch for the Transept of the Passion. This transept, now under scaffolding, above, is nearing completion.

OPPOSITE

A "Terrifying, Edible Beauty"
This phantasmagoric neo-Gothic Art-Nouveau jungle clusters around one of the portals of the church.

an opportunity to develop an intensely personal, and eventually quite a historical, building style. He began by being strikingly original in his textures and ornamental details, and went on to become startlingly—or appallingly, if you are one of the unconverted—original in his shapes, structures, interior spaces, and religious symbolism.

An important source of inspiration for his system of decoration was the Islamic and Iberian tradition of ceramic facing, best known in the form of the glazed pottery tiles, or *azulejos*, used on the exteriors and interiors of many Portuguese, Spanish, and Latin American buildings. In the early Casa Vicens the tiles are still conventional in shape, although unconventionally numerous (Gaudí's client, Manuel Vicens, was a tile manufacturer). In later works, partly perhaps because of the need to make the facing follow curved forms, irregular fragments are used; they form abstract patterns and waves of shimmering color on façades, roofs, chimneys, and spires and sometimes appear as molecules of bright color in the mortar between bricks.

The climax is reached at the Park Güell, where the gatehouse roofs and terrace benches look like a cross between a Pollock painting and a Disney cartoon and the ceiling of the many-columned portico is a kind of protosurrealist or proto-Dadaist collage that incorporates a doll's head and pieces of broken plates, cups, bottles, glass, and miscellaneous china.

Another source of inspiration was local, natural building material. Gaudí had more than one reason for preferring it to reinforced concrete, which from an engineering point of view was exactly the strong, plastic stuff his curved forms required and seemed to anticipate, and which was available after the mid-1890's—during, that is, the whole second half of his career. Traditional local material suited his neomedieval leanings, his nature worship, his handwork cult, and the labor skills most easily obtainable in Catalonia. But obviously one of his main reasons for liking it was the chance it gave him to compose with some of the freedom enjoyed by nonarchitectural artists, for he often joined his workers and even invented structural parts of his buildings on the spot.

His most characteristic walls are combinations of action architecture, abstract painting, and aleatory sculpture, animated by gestures in earth-colored brick, terra cotta, rough-cut stone, and a noble rubble that recalls Roman or Carolingian ruins. When he found blocks of stone uninteresting, he had them hammered and pitted by workmen until they reflected or absorbed sunlight in the way he wished.

For fences, railings, doors, and various unnamable ornaments his favorite material was iron, sometimes in a laminated or cast form, but usually wrought; and here again he had rich local resources from which to draw ideas. Ironwork had been a Catalan specialty since the Middle Ages, had been undergoing an exuberant renaissance in the nineteenth century, and was about to become what can be called the major Catalan contribution to modern art. It was not just a coincidence that Julio Gonzalez and Pablo Picasso, the pioneers of contemporary iron sculpture, were both from Barcelona.

In fact Gaudí himself was a third pioneer, even though some of his ironwork (along with some of his ceramic work) was done by assistants under his supervision. He pushed iron decoration into the cate-

PHOTOGRAPHS: ARCHIVO MAS, BARCELONA

Biological forms, including plaster leaf ceilings, top, iron flower fences, center, and masonry trees, above, give a writhing vivacity to Gaudí's work.

OPPOSITE

A Dragon in Cast Iron
This abstract monster snarls atop the gate of the Finca Güell, an estate in a suburb of Barcelona.

gory of expressionist iron sculpture and left the flat motifs of neo-medievalism and Modernismo far behind in many of the details of his perverse, tortured, bristling, and generally menacing metalwork for the Casa Vicens, the Finca Güell, the Casa Batlló, and the Casa Milá.

Generally menacing also are the nonmetal shapes he invented, not merely as ornaments but as functioning parts of his buildings. The chimneys and ventilator shafts on the Palacio Güell, the Casa Batlló, and the Casa Milá might be classified as the conspiratorial, the molluscan, the horripilant, and the fee-faw-fum. Roofs may suggest the backs of a herd of iridescent lizards, and façades may look like shelved collections of giant human organs. There is no really satisfactory explanation for these forms. The idea that Gaudí was simply converting the curved patterns of Art Nouveau into three-dimensional motifs scarcely accounts for the surrealist, or nightmare, quality. The idea that he was influenced by primitive sculpture is not supported by any hard evidence. That he was intent on imitating, or metamorphosing, nature is about all we can say—at least until depth psychologists go to work on the case.

The impulse toward dream biology is evident also in his structures (which often, of course, cannot really be separated from his strange shapes, any more than his strange shapes can really be separated from his strange textures and ornaments). The suggestion of solid flesh that is about to melt is often accompanied by a suggestion of tibiae, femurs, muscles, and something vaguely cartilaginous. The look of a prehistoric troglodyte dwelling may be accompanied by strong suggestions of petrified prehistoric trees.

But Gaudí was also a rationalist in his own eclectic and neomedieval fashion, particularly in his approach to the problems of architectural structures. He was greatly influenced at the start of his practice by Eugène Emmanuel Viollet-le-Duc's mechanistic theories, which explained the Gothic style as a skeletal system for conducting the thrusts of the arches and vaults from the ribs to the buttresses. He also admired the traditional Catalan technique of building curved membranes for vaults by laying tiles edge to edge and supporting them with stiffener ribs. Gradually he evolved his own constructional system, which might be described as neo-neo-Gothic—a continuation of Gothic from the point it had reached when it was halted by the Italian Renaissance. At the same time it was an anticipation in traditional materials of what engineers are doing today in reinforced and prestressed concrete.

The two most arresting features of this system are the parabolic arch, which can be seen to advantage in the Palacio Güell and the College of Santa Teresa de Jesús, and the inclined pier or column, which is used in a spectacular way in the galleries of the Park Güell and in the Colonia Güell chapel. The inclined pier was a result of his wish to redistribute thrusts so as to eliminate the flying buttress, which he dismissed as "a crutch." (Oddly, he affected a deep scorn for the Gothic architects and expressed admiration for the Greeks. Yet his only noticeable venture into neo-Greek is the hulking, leaning-columned Park Güell portico, which must be the sole example of comic Doric in architectural history.)

His interiors are what might be expected from his shapes and structures; they can be read, in the approved modern way, from the

outside. The crypt of the Colonia Güell, which is perhaps his masterpiece and was his laboratory for what he hoped to do at the Sagrada Familia, is like the belly of a giant insect. The surviving, or restored, apartments in the Casa Batlló and the Casa Milá are sections of warped space flooded with irrational light from unexpected windows. Their attics, in which his parabolic arches are dominant, produce the eerie effect of the interminable corridors tracked by the camera in *Last Year at Marienbad*.

For Gaudí, as for the devout in the Middle Ages, almost anything in the universe could be read as a religious symbol. The Sagrada Familia is symbolic not only in its profusion of figurative sculpture and its conventional Christian objects but also in its shapes and structures. The complete transept façade represents the Nativity; the three portals faith, hope, and charity; and the four minaretlike spires the apostles Barnabas, Jude, Simon, and Matthew (from left to right, as seen from the outside).

The other transept façade, now under construction, will stand for the Passion and will have relatively hard-edged geometrical shapes in order to symbolize the pain and desolation of the last hours before the Crucifixion and final sacrifice. The main façade will be that of the Glory of God; it will have seven columns to represent the seven deadly sins, seven doors to represent seven aspects of the religious service, a vaulted tunnel to represent hell, and so forth.

How should such a master builder be judged? Very severely, in the opinion of many orthodox modernists of the more or less functionalist school. For them he is an example of the folly of attempting to create serious architecture from nonarchitectural points of departure—by pushing painting, sculpture, and even literature into the realm of structure and practical planning. They point out that in spite of his liberal politics and genuine sympathy for the poor his work is sadly lacking in evidence of social conscience; more than half of it consists of luxurious town houses and apartments, and the remainder is mostly extravagant and unfinished religious architecture. His structural inventiveness is dismissed as play, since it was accompanied by a romantic rejection of the appropriate materials.

Professor Nikolaus Pevsner, in his standard work *Pioneers of Modern Design*, refers to Gaudí's art as "a flowering of Art Nouveau long after saner architects and designers had discarded it," and even implies that the whole business is just an instance of Spanish, or perhaps Catalan, illogicality. "Who," he asks, "would be ready to live in rooms of such curvy shapes, under roofs like the backs of dinosaurs, behind walls bending and bulging so precariously and on balconies whose ironwork might stab at you any moment? Who but an out-and-out aesthete or a compatriot of Gaudí and Picasso?"

Other authorities disagree. Henry-Russell Hitchcock calls the Sagrada Familia "perhaps the greatest ecclesiastical monument of the last hundred years" and the Casa Milá "the greatest masterpiece of the curvilinear mode of 1900." James Johnson Sweeney and José Luis Sert grant that their hero "does not really belong to this century" but praise him as "a born constructor" and a man of faith whose example can check our tendency "towards making technology an end instead of a means."

In Catalonia Gaudí has become material for Catalan patriotism,

JIM HUBBARD—PHOTO RESEARCHERS

ARCHIVO MAS, BARCELONA

ARCHIVO MAS, BARCELONA

Tumorous forms, opposite, engulf the windows of the Casa Batlló, a Barcelona apartment house remodeled by Gaudí between 1905 and 1907. The house, top, stands next to a stepped-gable house designed by one of Gaudí's friends. Center, a Casa Batlló dining room, with furniture by Gaudí, blends walls and ceiling into a continuous curve. In a salon, above, the swirling ceiling seems to grow out of the floor.

OVERLEAF

"Molluscan, Horripilant, and Fee-Faw-Fum"
So our author describes the elements of the roofscape of the Casa Milá, a Barcelona apartment house crowned by sinister squadrons of helmeted warriors.

ANNE E. HUBBARD—PHOTO RESEARCHERS

41

Recent echoes of Gaudí's highly expressionistic style of architecture include, top, Corbusier's sculptural chapel at Ronchamp, completed in 1954; center, John Johansen's cylindrical U.S. Embassy building, Dublin, 1964; and Eero Saarinen's winged TWA Terminal at New York's Kennedy Airport, 1962.

OPPOSITE

A Mace in the Sky

This strange spiked ornament, still another example of Gaudí's deliberate eccentricity, juts out from high up on the east façade of the Sagrada Familia.

for the tourist trade, and for scholarly research that almost rivals in scope the James Joyce industry in American universities. Municipal and provincial governments have voted funds for continued work on the Sagrada Familia; individual donors contribute generously on an annual collection day; and this year the church will attract, at the present rate, around two hundred thousand visitors. Yet, as I discovered on a recent trip, even in Barcelona opinions are divided. A merchant whose store affords a view of the Casa Batlló said to me, "Of course, he was not really a great architect. The proof is that he has had no successors." José Antonio Coderch, one of Spain's outstanding younger architects, was only cautiously approving: "The thing to imitate in Gaudí is not his forms, but the man—his integrity and his dedication to his profession."

My own opinion? Gaudí, I think, is an unusual instance of what can be called aesthetic imperialism—of the tendency in art and artists to annex everything. (He is by no means, of course, the only instance in the modern era. A Mondrian painting is not just a painting; it is an attempt to change our interior decoration, our houses, and even our philosophical outlook into something consonant with the Mondrian style. The Guggenheim is not so much a museum as an attempt by Wright to take over museums and museum visitors.) Gaudian leaning columns are not actually imitations of trees; they are attempts to annex trees to the Gaudian aesthetic.

When the architect argued, as apparently he frequently did, that man made straight lines and God made curves, what he actually meant, I suspect, was that God was to be annexed to the Gaudian empire. And if God had to accept the integration, there was certainly no reason to let apartment dwellers and other ordinary creatures preserve their independence and indulge their liking for practical planning. Big industry, big transport, and big government? These powers in modern society, which might prove hard to absorb, were not on the saintly Catalan's list of clients.

If I am even partly right, it would be proper for me to agree, reluctantly and approximately, with the functionalists, Pevsner, and the Barcelona merchant. Gaudí was not, after all, a really great architect. He lacked the ultimate humility of the really great ones, and their sense of architecture as a practical delight, a beautiful necessity. Somewhere inside the rough realist who enjoyed inclined piers and random rubble there was an arrogant 1890 dandy.

One might add, thinking of some of today's architectural trends, that one Gaudí in the twentieth century is quite enough. The world is full of people who are a bit more real than the Barcelona new class of the late nineteenth century and who are desperately in need of an architecture that serves, rather than dominates them.

However, having made these unavoidable judgments, I feel obliged to qualify them immediately. Granted, Gaudí was not a great architect. Granted also, one is enough. Can we not still say that he was an extraordinary man and a great artist? Evidently we can, and so the critical problem is to find an artistic category for him. Perhaps he ought simply to be called a great maker of habitable sculpture.

Roy McMullen is a regular contributor to HORIZON. *He wrote an article about Botticelli's* Primavera *for the Spring, 1968, issue.*

WHEN DOES A RIOT BECOME A REVOLUTION?

The senate house in flames; mobs roaring and rioting in the Forum, full of hate, hungry for blood—off they went looting and pillaging. Confronted by rival gangs, they fought and killed even in the *Sacra Via* itself, not once, but year after year as the Roman Republic crumbled. And the empire of Augustus only brought an uneasy peace. Social welfare, free food, and free fun kept the excesses down, but it required little—rumor, bribes, stirring oratory—to bring the mobs back into the streets.

When the capital of empire moved to the east, the mob was not lost. At Byzantium it rioted with equal violence, played on by oligarchs and factions in politics and religion. For centuries the mob rose and destroyed, tearing down buildings, pillaging, burning, and howling as it went.

In the summer of 1780, London erupted. By June 7, the city was a sea of flames; the prisons were broken open; the breweries were looted, and the gutters flowed with beer. Roman Catholic chapels and households were first desecrated, then wrecked, and finally burned. Among the rioters at least 285 were shot dead, 173 wounded, and 450 taken prisoner. These, the famous Gordon Riots, were unusual only in their extent. There had been wild rioting, burning, and looting in the 1760's and 70's; in 1733, 1736, and 1753 London had been at the mercy of mobs, as it had been time and time again during the previous century.

Not only in London but in towns throughout the kingdom generations of Englishmen had to learn to live with riots as they did with disease or death. It became a part of the nature of society. Nor was rioting an Englishman's vice; across the Channel they were just as violent. In the 1620's, 30's, and 40's France erupted in bloody riots that, in Normandy, finally turned into a peasants' war. For the rest of the century scarcely a year passed without mobs coming out in the streets of some provincial town or of Paris itself. They wreaked their vengeance on those whom they thought responsible for their misery.

The French Revolution changed the nature of European riots quite fundamentally. The mobs began to acquire more than a directing intelligence (they had rarely been without *that*) and to fall under the leadership of political strategists bent on using them for long-term ideological ends. Gradually the dispossessed and the frustrated acquired a deeper, a more ruthless, sense of identity, which encompassed violence, tragedy, pain, and even death for the sake of the future. And so the riot became an instrument of revolution. The European towns and countryside became even more violent in the nineteenth century; and England did, too—at least until 1850.

Things got better toward the end of the nineteenth century. Baron Haussmann drove his great boulevards through the riotous heart of Paris, providing excellent vistas for the rifle and, later, the machine gun and the tank. The weapons at the command of authority outdistanced the capacity of the mob to retaliate once the issue was joined. It was not until the 1920's and 30's that the riot was resuscitated by the paramilitary formation of the Fascists, the Nazis, and the *Action Française* on the one hand, and the Communist Party on the other. The military fanatics having been crushed, riots declined in Europe into protest that teetered along the border of violence but rarely broke into it.

Last spring Europe again burst into flames, with student riots from Colchester to Cracow. Although these riots were usually provoked by academic situations, they are being exploited by acute political leaders. The students have become a type of false

Reading the riot act in the 1870's: the tenant farmers of Scotland rioted for specific goals—security of tenure and lower rents. In 1886 they got them, with passage of the Crofters' Act.

© 1968 J. H. PLUMB

proletariat (a California professor has written "a student is a nigger"), and they are exploited as such. Attempts have been made—and with some success this past spring in France—to harness student idealism to the political programs of the working class. These recent riots in Europe belong to the tradition of both radical socialism and anarchism, but they are different in dimension from most American student riots and totally different in kind from the Negro rioting that America is experiencing.

The American riot is, as it were, the grandchild of the classical riot, which was bigger, more incoherent, more desperate—a deeper convulsion in the very bowels of society—than the recent disturbances in Europe. The present American experience is, more precisely, akin to the riots of *prerevolutionary* Europe, before the mobs became infiltrated with *political* agents and exploiters who turned the riot to social revolutionary ends. This stage may be beginning in America, however, and it could develop rapidly.

The classical riot was generally more than a sudden hysterical outburst of anguish and despair. While it lacked political leaders, it did not lack leadership. Usually there were journeymen, artisans, skilled craftsmen, modest yeomen farmers, who made up the hard core of the mob and led it to its targets. Their approach was often direct—to break open the granaries, to lower prices by threats of destruction, or to improve wages or even secure work.

But the root causes of most riots were economic and specific. They never aimed at overturning the structure of eighteenth-century society, any more than most rioting Negroes wished to overturn American capitalism and its social structure. The rioters were out to secure immediate benefits—economic, social, and *local*—not to start a revolution.

In England in the seventeenth century rioters tore down the hedges with which landowners had enclosed the peasants' common fields. In the eighteenth century they ripped up turnpike tollgates that taxed the movement of their goods. Riots worked more often than not. True, some rioters were caught, some hanged, some transported, some imprisoned; but the rioting mass escaped scot free, often with loot, and many times they were successful in winning their immediate, short-term aims.

So far the American urban riot is working in the same way as its historic counterparts. "A little early Easter shopping," said a Negro woman going off with a coat in the Washington looting that followed the murder of Martin Luther King. And apart from *immediate* gains there are practical and psychological gains, too.

The practical gain is quite simple. Large physical losses of property scare owners into action. An urgent sense that something positive must be done for Negroes immediately follows riot. It is a sobering fact that, as in the past so in the present, riots rarely fail; the rioters always win—not in the long term, of course, but in the short term.

The second gain is the release of social emotion. Before the nineteenth century the lower classes had little social hope. Societies, as far as they could see, never changed. There had been, and always would be, rich and poor. Riot, therefore, brought revenge as well as a windfall. Men burned their way across the countryside and into the cities in an orgiastic release of hatred and frustration.

To the overwhelming majority of Americans, black or white, rich or poor, a fundamental change in social structure is just as unthinkable as it was to eighteenth-century Englishmen. But as long as the conditions that lead to violence continue, the riot with its emotional release and its material windfalls and illusory social gains will go on and on, hot summer after hot summer, as it did for centuries in Europe.

In most countries of Europe riot eventually turned to revolution. In England, and England alone, riots faded into insignificance in the nineteenth century. France in 1789 led the way; it proved through the Reign of Terror that social change and political power could be achieved through mobs harnessed to a political ideology of social hope—a lesson never forgotten by the French or by the countries to which they exported their ideas. England nearly followed suit—right up to 1850, revolution was possible. Then Britain was saved by the enormous affluence of its industrial revolution in full spate—supported by a dependent and exploited empire—and by the creation of a pattern of social hope for all classes through universal elementary education and full political participation. There were other and more complex factors at work, but these were the primary ones.

America is, in a sense, entering a political phase curiously akin to that of Europe in the nineteenth century, a world of savage social conflict and possible revolutionary turmoil. Which way will riot develop? Will it be molded by revolutionary leaders into a revolutionary movement, dedicated to social change, and if need be to civil war? Or will the riots fade away, as they did in Britain, by the creation of true, not false, social hope and by full, not spurious, political participation? I am not suggesting that the British governing classes made that social hope easily realizable, or that full political participation quickly prized their hands from the wheels of government. Of course not. But classes, like individuals, leap at a glimmer of real hope.

The hope must be real. If time and time again it proves illusory, then the looting will stop, the rioters will become disciplined, ferocious, dedicated, willing to die by the tens of thousands so that they can kindle an unquestionable spark of hope in the hearts of their own people. They will start fighting not for the present but the future.

The Incomparable Enfantin: A Moral Tale

How he sought
the perfect woman
to beget
the future Saviour.
How he lost
faith and went into
the desert.
And how he came to
a happy ending
as General Manager
of the
P.-L.-M. railroad

Familiar enough in history are the mighty rulers who have attained godhead and commanded the worship of their subjects. Unique, however, is the case of Le Père Enfantin, who, after a stage as deity, became General Manager of an important railroad.

Barthélemy Prosper Enfantin emerged from a humility suitable for the origin of divinity. He was born in Paris in 1796, the illegitimate son of an impoverished banker. A brilliant student, he gained entry to the Ecole Polytechnique, the government school of engineering. After only a year, in 1814 his course was interrupted by the fall of Napoleon. He became a wine merchant. His powers of persuasion proving remarkable, he explored sales possibilities in Germany, Switzerland, and Holland. He spent two years in St. Petersburg as an employee of a French banker, thus learning the ways of finance. With a group of radical French expatriates he learned also to cogitate loftily on political economy and social theory, the making of a new world through the overturn of the old. He returned to France, worked as a bank teller (later becoming a director), and addressed proposals for fiscal reform to the government. And he became a convert to the theories of Saint-Simon.

Claude Henri de Rouvroy, Comte de Saint-Simon, was the founder of French socialism. A touching idealist who fought for liberty in the American Revolution, he demanded a total reorganization of society on a basis of economics. Production of goods should replace landholding, for "the social aim is to produce things useful to life." Industrialists should take the place of nobles; scientists, artists, and philosophers, instead of churchmen, should direct society, with the well-being of the proletariat as their aim. His fol-

The Parisian prophet Le Père Enfantin was sketched in 1832 in the uniform—white trousers, blue jacket—that he designed for his disciples, who helped him in founding Saint-Simon's socialist utopia in France.

lowers preached that the inheritance of wealth should be forbidden, the gold base of money abolished, women emancipated, and a kind of United Nations established. Saint-Simon proclaimed: "From each according to his capacities, to each according to his works."

In 1825 Saint-Simon died, and Enfantin, along with a few other chief disciples, inherited his prophetic robe. Enfantin devoted himself to spreading and improving the master's doctrines. He helped found a newspaper, gave public lectures, and rented a dilapidated residence in the rue Monsigny, near the center of Paris. There a group of adepts lived; and there resorted the social-minded, the forward-lookers, and the merely curious. "The family in the rue Monsigny was like a glowing hearth," remembered Louis Blanc, famous in the history of social reform. "Many among the audience listened with a smile on their lips, and raillery in their eyes; but after the orator had spoken for a while there would be one feeling among his hearers of astonishment mixed with admiration."

Enfantin's heady doctrine was in part economic. Labor should gain all its rights and own the means of production. Banks, founded by the idle for idlers, should be organized by and for the workers. His doctrine was also social. Privileges of birth and wealth should be abolished; merit alone should admit men to power. Communal life should succeed to family grouping. Scholars, the new rulers and priests, would suppress poverty-breeding competition, war-breeding nationalism, the excesses of individual initiative. Women, who are clearly the equals or the superiors of men, should be freed from their vows of obedience and fidelity, which lead only to oppression, adultery, and prostitution. Each sex should have absolute liberty to determine its own fate; temporary marriages should be as legitimate and holy as permanent ones. Finally, Enfantin's doctrine was a metaphysic and a religious faith. Men are in communion with one another,

with the universe. Matter as well as spirit is divine; the flesh is holy. We shall transmigrate into better bodies and share in a future life, though personality will not persist. "The dead have no other tomb than the living." God, obviously, is neither male nor female; He-She is an androgyne. The Couple, merging self with nonself, is the sacred unit. Thus Enfantin, *le Père*, must find *la Mère*, to form the priest-couple. Their mating, a symbol of social union, would bring a new revelation.

Much of the history of Enfantin's movement consisted in the hunt for the Mother, the Female Messiah. She was sought afar, not only in France, but in Turkey, Egypt, and America. Many candidates appeared, but the Father was always obliged to announce, after testing, that this again was not his destined bride. While awaiting her he could not accept the bonds of human marriage. This announcement brought grief particularly to Adèle Morlane, mother of his son. Enfantin treated both mother and son very badly, according to the standards of Christian society, which are outworn, to be sure.

Enfantin was a great preacher of his Word. Everyone mentions his personal beauty. He was tall, elegant, with light chestnut hair, fine features, and compelling eyes. He threw on all "a spell of enchantment," said Louis Blanc. In speech he would ascend from a plane of actuality to an empyrean of poetic but cloudy imagination. He could send an audience into convulsive ecstasies. One enthusiast was filled with the Holy Ghost and prophesied incoherently. Some auditors fainted and were removed without interruption to the proceedings. A magistrate had a stroke at one of the meetings and died, luckily leaving his property to the movement.

The faithful acclaimed Enfantin as the Chief of Humanity, the Living Law, the successor of Moses, Jesus, and Saint-Simon. Said one: "Father, I believe in you as I believe in the sun!" Many distinguished visitors sat in the

By MORRIS BISHOP

Abolition of servants at Enfantin's community, as seen by a skeptic: the brethren fumble with the household chores while Enfantin woos a lady disciple.

hall: the critic Sainte-Beuve, the father of Rosa Bonheur, the poet Heine (who dedicated a book to Enfantin). Berlioz came; Liszt played the piano for waltzing. The composer Félicien David was a total convert. John Stuart Mill and Thomas Carlyle wrote their approval from England.

Early in 1832 Enfantin's mother died, leaving him a good-sized house set in ample gardens and grounds in Ménilmontant, on the eastern outskirts of Paris. (The site is marked by the tiny rue des Saint-Simoniens.) Le Père, discouraged by a falling-out with another leader of the movement, announced that forty of the faithful, all male, would take up residence in Ménilmontant and there await the promised Mother. "I can no longer be the mother who cradles her children and soothes them gently with her caresses. You are men, and I wish to be the Father of men." All the chosen were obliged to take a vow of chastity. Some indignant wives forced defections from the forty; others were left destitute. But most of the adepts submitted to the divine command and declared their marriages void.

The Father designed a uniform for his apostles—white trousers in summer (blue in winter), a red-bordered white vest that laced up the back (symboliz-

ing man's need of a companion, even to dress him), a blue tunic, a floating scarf, and a red toque. Across Enfantin's breast was embroidered LE PERE. Above the new home floated a flag with horizontal stripes of white, violet, and red, representing religion, science, and industry. The schedule was military—reveille at 5 A.M., lights out at 9:30 P.M. There were no servants, for domestic work was branded as a form of slavery. Everyone took his turn at the housework, to the amusement of Paris cartoonists. Courses were given in astronomy, geography, geology, and music; and all took a hand in preparing the new gospel, *Le Livre Nouveau*, which would fix the dogma and practice of the faith. (The book was never, in fact, published.) Enfantin happily indulged his taste for bold reforms. He changed the names of the weekdays: Monday became Saint-Simon; Saturday, Le Père; Sunday, La Mère, Mother's Day. He planned a New City, which would take the form of the human body—at the head, the temples and academies of priests and scholars; in the stomach, factories and workshops; in the legs, promenades and parks; at the feet, dance halls.

Throngs of visitors were attracted to the biweekly open house at Ménilmontant. All danced, sang the new hymns, and listened to the moving but

disturbing discourses of the Father. The authorities were alarmed, recognizing the workings of a revolutionary spirit.

Enfantin and his chief aides were charged with "outrage against public morality" and arrested. The trial was the delight of Paris. The Father asked to be defended by women lawyers; since none existed, he acted as his own counsel. After a vain attempt to hypnotize judges and jury with his powerful eye, he proclaimed that he was sent by God, who is father and mother of all. "My mission is not ended! God has not made incarnate his Word in man for a second time, only to crucify him again between thieves! God does not repeat himself!" Nevertheless the jury found him guilty; with two others, he was condemned to a year in jail.

He found his martyrdom very tolerable. He was comfortably lodged in a de luxe political prison. He collected a large library and had plenty of leisure for his literary work. The faithful loaded him with dainties. The warden even asked him to dine, but he refused on a point of etiquette, because the invitation arrived only half an hour before the function.

But on his release, in 1833, he found his movement tottering. Far from daunted, he proposed to visit Egypt: to find *la Mère*, to convert the Egyptians to Saint-Simonism, and to build a canal across the Isthmus of Suez. The project of a canal, already thousands of years old, appealed to the engineer in him. Since he saw things in the large, he announced as his purpose the reconciliation of the Orient and the Occident. But money for such a grandiose enterprise was lacking; it was barely sufficient for boat fare.

Enfantin and twelve followers, including some engineers, disembarked in Egypt in apostolic destitution. They were succored by the French colony and were presented to the pasha, who found their scheme of canal building terrifyingly expensive. (But Ferdinand de Lesseps, the French consul, listened and took notes.) The pasha rejected the canal but gladly accepted the newcomers' technical aid in the constructing of a dam across the Nile, just below Cairo. With Enfantin as director, a corps of Saint-Simonian polytechnicians sent out from France labored on the dam, apparently with competence, until work was interrupted by a raging plague.

Enfantin seems then to have been sobered, disillusioned, a prey to self-doubt. "I am beginning to be a little less of a monster," he wrote to a lady friend. Wearing native dress, he spent a year in Upper Egypt awaiting a revelation, visiting the antiquities, shooting crocodiles, and conducting intimate

Saint-Simonians help each other dress in vests laced at the back.

anthropological investigations among the native women.

He returned to France early in 1837, after three years' absence, to find his reform movement in ruins and the Ménilmontant estate foreclosed. He was now forty years old, unemployed, and in most men's eyes unemployable. He sought a government post, suggesting that of Minister of Commerce and Public Works. Persuaded that reform is best begun at the top rather than with the lowly, he invented the "royal apostolate." He would first convert the emperor of Austria, a priestly ruler, and then work down. But somehow he could never establish contact. He succeeded, finally, in joining a scientific mission to Algeria but eventually lost the post because his report failed to deal with the subjects assigned him.

Thus at the end of the 1830's he relapsed into obscurity. Apparently he was running some sort of an express or forwarding service in Lyon. Such would be the normal end of the illuminate, the fantast, the aging outcast god. We imagine him conducting a little, perilous business, living in a dusty attic, clutching at chance acquaintances to tell his unsought tales. He would seem to have reached a destined outcome—failure. But on the contrary the defeated demigod found a resurrection among his human brothers.

It happened that Lyon was a center of railroad building. The early railroads of France were local lines, joining city to nearby city. Enfantin, whose conceptions were seldom less than cosmic, imagined a great trunk line from Le Havre to Marseilles joining sea to sea, co-operating with a Suez Canal, and challenging England's control of transport to the East. His proposals gained him public notice; he found himself the representative of the *Lyonnais* with the great bankers of Paris. He worked hand in hand with the Rothschilds, Pereires, Laffittes, Hottingers. They were dreamers, too; they welcomed his bold ideas. He was the chief

Utopian railroad magnate, Enfantin sits in sedate comfort in 1853.

promoter of the Paris-Lyon-Méditerranée line. In 1845 he became a director and in 1856 *Administrateur*, or General Manager.

Desirous of finding consistency in human behavior, we look for the fatal flaw, for the pathetic absurdity that would reveal itself in Enfantin's conduct and topple him into foredestined failure. He disappoints us. During business hours, at least, he was totally the businessman, prudent and competent. But he never disavowed the Saint-Simonian faith. He made the relations between management and labor of the P.-L.-M. a model for their time, with workers' mutual-aid funds, schools, libraries, and a museum. He proposed a *crédit intellectuel*, a central fund of knowledge, an intellectual bank, which would make loans of knowledge for production and provide subsidies for young men "who need six thousand francs before they can earn a sou."

He died, rich and full of honors, in the year 1864.

Evidently an ex-demigod can succeed in business. But at a cost. Monsieur l'Administrateur Enfantin lost the divinity of Le Père Enfantin. And he never found the Female Messiah.

This is the second in a series of brief biographical escapades by Morris Bishop. The first was published in Spring, 1968.

How Do I Know You Mean What You Mean?

If a man thinks in one language, he thinks one way; in another language, another way. So said Benjamin Lee Whorf, who explained why man's thought is a prisoner of his tongue

Language is that marvelous instrument that lifts man above all other living things. No other animal possesses anything that even remotely resembles a language ("Polly wants a cracker" conveys to the imitating parrot only meaningless sounds). Language makes the man—but it is also becoming increasingly clear that language serves as a barrier between groups of men. The problem goes much deeper than mere difficulties of translation, for it questions the very way we perceive and experience the world around us. Linguistically speaking, man is not born free. Our linguistic minds were made up for us from the day we were born. We have inherited our culture's particular habits of perception and expression, and these particular habits often differ markedly from those inherited by people in different cultures.

Nature bombards us with sounds, smells, sights, and other sensations. All humans are born with the sensory and motor potential to detect them, and so all humans should be able to report exactly what their senses tell them. But do they? Imagine two U.S. Forest Service employees, one a white American and the other a Navaho Indian, riding the range together in Arizona. They notice a broken wire fence. The white speaker of English will report back to his superior that "a fence is broken at such-and-such a place." He is content that he has perceived the situation well and reported it conscientiously. The Navaho would undoubtedly consider such a report vague and perhaps even meaningless. His report will be much different, because he will follow the channels of perception demanded of him by his language.

First of all, the Navaho speaker must point out that the fence belongs to a category of inanimate things; this immediately clears up any possible misunderstanding that something happened to a living creature, such as a fence lizard. The verb he selects will indicate that the fence material was long and thin and thus presumably wire (the white ranger's report failed to mention whether the fence was made of wood or wire). The Navaho then must choose among several verb forms that tell whether the fence consisted of one strand, a few, or many strands of wire. Similarly, the act of breaking will be reported with much greater precision. The Navaho speaker must choose between two different words that tell us the fence was broken either by a human act or by some nonhuman agency such as a windstorm; his choice of words will probably also indicate the way in which the fence was broken. And, finally, his verb will tell us whether or not the fence is presently moving (being whipped by the wind, perhaps, or carried downstream by a flood).

The Navaho's report will probably be no longer than the white American's, but it will make numerous distinctions that it never occurred to the conscientious white man to make, because his language does not demand them. The Navaho's report would translate as something like this: "A fence (which belongs to a particular category of inanimate things) (of long and thin wire) (made of many strands) is (moved to a position) (where it came to rest) broken (by nonhumans) (in a certain way)."

Language does more than merely blind its speaker to certain perceptions; by an opposite influence it directs the speaker's attention into certain habitual patterns of thought. In the Arctic the Eskimo often travels through an environment in which no horizon separates earth from sky, where the winds rise and snow blots out all perspective. A study some years ago of the Aivilik Eskimos, who live north of Hudson Bay, showed that they sometimes travel for hundreds of miles in such conditions. They can do so because they unconsciously perceive their environment, not as a collection of points and lines that fill a space, but as interrelationships among snow, wind, ice cracks, contours, and so forth.

It is not that the Eskimo has keener senses than we do. It is just that his

By PETER FARB

language has bestowed on him different channels along which to track his observations, and different categories in which to place them. The many discriminations his language accustoms him to make about snow and ice and wind enable him to survive in a very harsh environment in which we would soon perish. (By the same token an Eskimo speaker undoubtedly would find it difficult to detect without training the distinctions a variety of our words make about a horse—"mare," "stallion," "pony," "bay," "paint," "chestnut," "appaloosa," and so on.)

Vocabulary alone is the least important distinction made by different languages; what really matters is the totality of the patterns and internal structures of the language. It is no wonder that an Eskimo should have a wide variety of words for the different kinds and conditions of seals, which can be translated as "a young spotted seal," "a female harbor seal," "a swimming male ribbon seal," and so forth. But it is a surprise to learn that the Eskimo does *not* include in the same category "a giant bearded seal" —even though every mammalogist can prove anatomically that it belongs there. If we inquire into Eskimo culture, we learn that it makes the same distinction the Eskimo language does: all the other kinds of seals can be killed by individual hunters, but the giant bearded seal can be killed only by cooperating bands of hunters.

Our culture categorizes seals according to their biology; Eskimo culture, by the degree of social organization needed to kill them. Every culture similarly categorizes experience through its language. It has to, because every minute of the day an individual is bombarded by so many sensory impressions that only by compartmentalizing them in a few categories can he detect patterns. If he took notice of every detail struggling for his attention, he would know only a tremendous number of isolated events, which would never recur in exactly the same way. So it is clear that a child learning

his native language learns more than a set of vocal skills. He unconsciously learns the way his own group selects from the sensory bombardment and categorizes what it has selected.

Ancient folk beliefs long assumed such a connection between a people's individuality and its language. The Hebrews believed that their language was a holy vehicle that God had awarded to them alone. The ancient Greeks gave the label "barbarians" (that is, speakers of an unintelligible tongue that sounded like *bar-bar*) to those foreigners whom the gods had denied the gift of the Greek language. But no one thought scientifically about the matter until the German philologist and diplomat Wilhelm von Humboldt became the first to clearly state—in his "Essay on the Character of the American Verb"—that the structure of a language expresses the inner life and knowledge of its speakers. In another essay, published after his death in 1835, he said that "man lives with the world about him principally, indeed . . . exclusively, as language presents it."

Franz Boas of Columbia University revived the idea when he edited in 1911 a massive study of American Indian languages and proposed that the speakers of the different languages be studied psychologically and culturally. His presentation of a number of exotic American Indian languages showed that each language was its own closed system, which could be unlocked by linguistic analysis. Only a few linguists showed any interest, and the

study of the interrelationship of language and culture waned—until 1939, when a remarkable amateur linguist, Benjamin Lee Whorf of Hartford, Connecticut, started publishing the results of his intensive study of the language of the Hopi Indians of Arizona.

Whorf's brilliant analysis of Hopi, which demanded about eight years of hard work, placed the old folk beliefs about language and culture on a scientific basis; it also supported the idea that man is a prisoner of his language. Whorf stated that the structure of a language "is not merely a reproducing instrument for voicing ideas but rather is itself the shaper of ideas, the program and guide for the individual's mental activity, for his analysis of impressions, for his synthesis of his mental stock in trade. . . . We dissect nature along lines laid down by our native languages."

When Whorf died in 1941, only forty-four years of age, he had hardly begun work on the book he had hoped to write about his discoveries. But he did leave behind him some very articulate essays in a number of scholarly journals. They were collected in one volume and finally published in 1956 as *Language, Thought, and Reality*. Since the book's publication Whorf's influence has spread from a small group of linguists to specialists in such fields as anthropology, psychology, and sociology. His views are widely discussed in communications theory, in the new field of "proxemics" (man's use of space), and in the behavioral sciences; and his methodology has had a great influence on the whole field of structural linguistics.

There is no general agreement about what to call Whorf's theories of language and culture, and at one time or another they have been referred to as "the Whorf hypothesis," "linguistic relativity," "psycholinguistics," "metalinguistics," "ethnolinguistics," and so on. Whatever the label, there is no doubt that in the past decade or so Whorf has forced us to re-evaluate our traditional thinking about language,

COURTESY OF MRS. CELIA WHORF

Benjamin Lee Whorf

cognition, and cultural behavior.

When Whorf graduated from the Massachusetts Institute of Technology in 1918 as a chemical engineer, he had never displayed any particular interest in language. A few months later he went to work at the home office of the Hartford Fire Insurance Company; he stayed with that company until his death, serving as a conscientious employee at the junior executive level. Whorf first became interested in language because of his fundamentalist religious beliefs. The discrepancy between the Bible and modern scientific evidence, he came to believe, might be more apparent than real and might be due to mistranslations of the Bible. So in 1924 he began to study Hebrew.

His curiosity about language already aroused, he learned that there existed in a Hartford library a very extensive, but little-used, collection of publications about American Indian culture and language that had been assembled in the previous century. Whorf got in the habit of stopping by the library after work; he began the study of the Aztec materials in 1926 and of the Mayan language two years later. And as early as 1928 his translations became known to several professional linguists; they resulted in a modest grant that enabled Whorf and his wife to visit Mexico in 1930 to study first-hand the living speakers of Nahuatl, the language of the Aztecs.

The next year one of America's most distinguished linguists, Edward Sapir, came to Yale from the University of Chicago, and Whorf enrolled in his course on American Indian languages. Sapir himself had already speculated about the relationship of language and culture. In 1929 he had written the following: "Human beings do not live in the objective world alone, nor alone in the world of social activity as ordinarily understood, but are very much at the mercy of the particular language which has become the medium of expression for their society. . . . The worlds in which different societies live are distinct worlds, not merely the same world with different labels attached."

Sapir convinced Whorf to switch from the study of Nahuatl to a related language spoken by the Hopi Indians of Arizona. Sapir obtained another small grant for Whorf and also put him in touch with a Hopi Indian who was working in New York. Whorf and his Hopi informant alternated visits between New York and Hartford, and in this way Whorf worked steadily at his analysis of the language. Not until 1938 did he visit a Hopi reservation and meet the people whose language he knew better than any other white and probably better than most Hopis.

Whorf was a slender, vigorous man with quick movements and dark, intelligent eyes, who looked, according to a friend, as if he were walking through life with a constant question on his face. Perhaps the most amazing thing about him was that in spite of his all-consuming search for the hidden meanings of language he never resented the full schedule of work at his insurance office. As his reputation as a linguist spread, he was offered academic posts, even though he lacked an advanced degree. But he turned down all offers in order to maintain his amateur status. (There must have been something particularly bracing about the insurance business in those years, for in the same area there also blossomed, largely unnoticed, two other geniuses who spent their days at insurance company jobs and their evenings and weekends creating—the composer Charles Ives and the poet Wallace Stevens.)

Whorf's insurance work was not completely unrelated to his study of the language and culture of the Hopi. It had been his job to analyze hundreds of reports of the circumstances surrounding the start of fires. Over and over again he came to the conclusion that the basic cause of the fires had been certain assumptions the people who started the fires were led by their language to make. For example, he dis-covered that workers at one plant made no attempt to protect a limestone compound from heat; to their surprise it caught fire and burned vigorously. The English language had led the workers to be careless around limestone because the word ends in "-stone," and everyone who speaks English knows that stones are noncombustible.

From 1939 on Whorf started to put his linguistic theories into written form. A year later he learned that he was dying of lung cancer; despite increasing weakness, he continued to work until the time of his death. *The New York Times* printed a brief editorial about his amateur status in a complex specialty, the language of the Aztec, but never mentioned his theories of the interrelationship of language and culture.

In his studies Whorf had found many contrasts between Hopi and the European languages (including English). Among the more important were these:

Plurality. In English we use the plural both for "five men" and "five days." But "men" and "days" by no means fit the same category. We can see with our eyes a group of five men standing on a street corner, but how can we perceive five days? To do so we have to conjure up an imaginary picture, perhaps one of recurring circles of time of equal length. The Hopi does no such thing. He does not rely on his imagination to provide him with plurals that do not exist in reality. He would never use a description of a cycle—"days," "hours," "minutes," "years," or other units of time—in the same way that he would use an aggregate noun ("men"). His language is much neater; there is a separate category altogether for cycles. For him time is not plural, but instead it merely has duration. The Hopi equivalent for "He stayed five days" would be "He stayed until the sixth day."

Quantity. In English we have nouns that refer to individual things with definite outlines ("a tree," "a ball," "a man") and also mass nouns that refer to things that lack sharp boundaries ("water," "wood," "meat"). These mass nouns seem to cause some unconscious uneasiness in us. For one thing, we often drop the articles "a" or "the" before them. For another, we feel the need to limit these mass nouns by introducing before them the names of containers and body types: "*a glass of* water," "*a stick of* wood," "*a piece of* meat." But such limitations do not solve the problem, because all we have really done is to shift our perception from the water to the glass in which it may be contained.

The Hopi language handles the problem of mass nouns by not having them. It can refer to the concept of water in general just as well as we can in English, but it does so through its verbs. Its individual nouns, then, can efficiently imply indefiniteness of outline or size, but not total lack of it, as our mass nouns do. The Hopi noun itself does the work of implying the limitation: *nguhmni* means "a (quantity of) corn flour." And Hopi also categorizes "water" in different ways. For example, it has one category for the usually small amounts under human control (such as water in a glass) and another for the often larger amounts of water in nature (such as that in a lake, or even dew).

Tenses. English tends to stand time in a row as three units of past, present, and future; we imagine an event as occurring someplace along this row. Hopi has done away with tenses. The Hopi speaker's verb does not indicate the past, present, or future of the event itself. Whereas we would say "He is running" as an example of the present tense, the Hopi speaker would say this in any one of at least five ways, depending upon the context: "I know that he is running now." "I know that he is running now even though you cannot see him." "I remember that I saw him running and presume he is still running." "I expect that he is running and will come." "I know that he is running (that is, for the track team)."

Duration and intensity. English expresses duration and intensity by using such words as "long," "short," "great," "slow," and "quick" for duration and "large," "much," "sharp," and "high" for intensity. We are so much in the habit of using such words that we have forgotten that every one of them refers to size, shape, number, or motion— they are, in other words, metaphors of space. We spatialize by our imagination qualities that our senses tell us are nonspatial, and we resort to these spatial metaphors even in the simplest situations: "He *slowly grasped* the *thread* of the story, but its *level* was too *high,* and so he differed *widely at last,* thinking the *views* were *a lot* of nonsense." Hopi is equally striking in the absence of such metaphors of imaginary space.

Whorf found that, whereas we think in terms of time and space, the Hopi language gives each speaker a very particular analysis of reality in terms of *events.* The critical question now is: do Hopi Indians and people speaking European languages show in their respective behavior that their cultures unconsciously conceptualize reality in these different ways?

In the case of time, it is for us a commodity that is measurable and occurs between fixed points. Time can be "wasted" or "saved." An army fighting a rear-guard action can "buy" time, and a television station can "sell" time to an advertiser. We keep records, diaries, accounts, and histories; we plan the future with schedules, programs, and budgets. Our whole economic system emphasizes wages for time worked, rent for time occupied, interest for the length of time money is loaned, depreciation for the time something is used, premiums for fixed times of insurance.

Hopi culture has none of these beliefs about time. Time is not measurable. Plant seed, and corn will grow. The length of time the growing takes is not the important thing, but rather the way in which the events of growth inevitably follow the act of planting. The Hopi is concerned that the sequence of events in building a house be in the correct order, not how soon the whole job is completed. That is why the building of a Hopi house, adobe brick by brick, may go on for years.

Similarly, English and Hopi differ very much in their attitudes about space. The extent to which we are preoccupied by space was pointed up by an anthropologist who went through an English dictionary and noted all the words that had spatial connotations, such as "together," "distant," "under," "linked," adjacent," and "congruent." They totaled nearly five thousand words—about 20 per cent of all the words in that dictionary. We constantly speak of imaginary space in words that connote real space. To us, a "church" is a building with a tall steeple; it can also be a particular religious denomination. But a Hopi would find senseless the statement by a religious convert that he "entered the Methodist church." By the same token, the Hopi has difficulty picturing the places the missionaries assure him are "heaven" and "hell."

The anthropologist Edward T. Hall* of Northwestern University tells of a Hopi he knew who decided to build his house in the middle of a road. By our standards—and so Hall informed him —the Hopi was guilty of usurping space; that is because European languages teach us to think of space as occurring along lines and points. He seemed amazed both at Hall's reproach and at Hall's conception of space.

Whorf's hypothesis has been greeted enthusiastically by some scholars and attacked or treated warily by others. Whorf hits us where it hurts the most: as Freud did, he impugns our ability to be objective. He throws into doubt the rationality of our everyday decisions. He suggests that all our lives we have been tricked by the English language— and it is small consolation for us to know that the Hopi has also been tricked, although in a different way.

One of the earliest attacks upon Whorf was based upon the cultures of the Hopi and the Navaho. Detractors

*An article about Edward T. Hall by William Kloman appears in the Autumn, 1967, Horizon.

pointed out that these two Indian groups, living side by side in Arizona, share a common culture—yet their languages come from completely different families. Such a seemingly devastating attack forced anthropologists to examine the Hopi and Navaho cultures more closely. They concluded that despite the external similarities, the world views of the two groups actually were far apart—as predicted by the differences in their language families.

Since then more sophisticated experiments have been performed, and some of them tend to support Whorf's hypothesis. The Southwest Project in Comparative Psycholinguistics has devised some particularly elaborate tests. One of them used as subjects more than one hundred Navaho children, who were carefully selected from the same small area of the reservation and were similar in family background, in age, and in all other aspects of culture and environment—with only one variable. The sole variable was language. The children were divided into two groups: one spoke only Navaho, or spoke it predominantly, and the other spoke some English.

The experimenters had already carefully studied the Navaho language and knew that a speaker must use a different verb according to the shape of the object about which he is speaking. A Navaho cannot say simply and vaguely, "I handle." The verb must indicate if what he is handling is long and flexible, like fence wire; if it is long and rigid, like a stick, he must use a different verb form; if it is flat and flexible, like cloth, the speaker must use yet another verb form; and so on. Navaho-speaking children use these different verb forms for shapes with unerring correctness even at age three or four.

Here was a perfect opportunity to test the Whorf hypothesis, for it predicts that the Navaho-speaking children should unconsciously categorize objects on the basis of shape, while the children who spoke some English would

---

"I AM GOING" IN NAVAHO

To the early explorers from Europe, the American Indian languages were thought to be "primitive," because only the Aztec and Mayan languages in Mexico were written. Actually, no "primitive" language has yet been found in the world. Most of these exotic languages are more complex than English, and often superior to it. The Navaho language, for example, is much more precise in many ways than English. The vague statement in English "I am going" is impossible to make in Navaho. First of all, the Navaho verb stem would indicate one of the following:

"I am going on foot."
"I am going on horseback."
"I am going by wagon."
"I am going by boat."
"I am going by airplane."

Say that the method of motion selected is horseback. The Navaho speaker will now give further information, choosing from the following verb forms:

"I am going by horseback at a walk."
"I am going by horseback at a trot."
"I am going by horseback at a gallop."
"I am going by horseback at a run."

Now the Navaho speaker must make another category of distinctions. "Going" is much too indefinite for him, and no such simple word exists. The act of going is differentiated into "getting ready to go," "going along right now," "almost arriving at my destination," "returning from my destination"—and about five other possible choices.

The question is not whether such fine distinctions *can* be made in English. As you see, I did manage to make them by the use of cumbersome circumlocutions for the one or two words the Navaho would use. The point is that habitually I do not provide all of that information, say, to my wife; my culture does not demand it of me, neither does my language. I tell her that "I am going to the store." If she wants to know whether I will walk or drive the car, she will have to ask me. She will also have to ask how soon I will be leaving, whether or not I expect the trip to be a long one, whether I am going to the store directly or whether I will stop off someplace first, whether I will stay or will return at once. A Navaho-speaking wife never has to nag.

—P.F.

---

be less likely to do so. A test was devised that presented each child with a pair of objects that differed in both shape and color; the child was then presented with a third object to match that was similar to each of the other two in only one characteristic. For example, the children were shown a *yellow rope* and a *blue stick*. They were then asked to match one of these objects with a *blue rope*. About 70 per cent of the Navaho-speaking children matched on the basis of shape—that is, they matched the *yellow rope* and the *blue rope*. In contrast about 60 per cent of the children who spoke some English matched on the basis of color—the

blue stick with the *blue rope*. Nine more experiments of increasing complexity of choice were performed, and there was a consistent tendency for the Navaho-speakers to categorize according to shape and the children with a knowledge of English to categorize according to color. Whorf's belief that the structure of a language unconsciously influences behavior in categorizing experience seems to have been supported by these tests.

A point might be made against the Whorf hypothesis by suggesting that Whorf, as well as precursors such as Von Humboldt, Boas, and Sapir, all worked with American Indian languages and that the hypothesis might apply solely to them. A few years ago a rather elegant test was carried out that showed the applicability of the hypothesis to Japanese, which is completely unrelated to any American Indian language. Once again an attempt was made to keep all conditions of culture and behavior constant except for language. An ideal group of test subjects was located in San Francisco: Japanese girls who had married American soldiers. Each was completely bilingual. English was used in talking to their husbands and children and neighbors and for everyday occupations such as shopping. Japanese was spoken whenever the girls got together to reminisce, gossip, and discuss the news from home. Each Japanese woman was truly occupying two linguistic worlds. According to the prediction of the Whorf hypothesis, each girl should act differently in each of these linguistic worlds.

The actual testing consisted of two visits by a trained bilingual Japanese interviewer to each girl. At the first interview he spoke to them only in Japanese; at the second interview the same test questions were asked in English. The results were quite remarkable. One test, for example, consisted of giving the girls only the first part of various sentences. During the visit in which only Japanese was spoken the sentences were completed in that language; at the visit in which English was spoken the very same sentences were completed in English. Here is one example of the different ways the same woman completed the same sentences —depending on which language she was speaking.

1) When my wishes conflict with my family's . . .
   (in Japanese) . . . it is a time of great unhappiness.
   (in English) . . . I do what I want.

2) I will probably become . . .
   (in Japanese) . . . a housewife.
   (in English) . . . a teacher.

3) Real friends should . . .
   (in Japanese) . . . help each other.
   (in English) . . . be very frank.

Clearly the world views of the same women underwent drastic changes, depending upon the language world each was in at the time.

While some specialists are still disputing the Whorf hypothesis, many others are finding it a fruitful field of study. But as enthusiasm for Whorf's work grows, there is a danger that we may be led into ideas or conclusions that he never made, and in fact may have specifically warned against. One such simplistic conclusion is that if we can change people's words, we can change their ideas. Everyone knows that an advertising campaign often stands or falls on its slogan, sometimes merely on a single word (a lengthy article might be written just about the efficacy of the word "pure"). Many people also believe, probably with some accuracy, that the American Medical Association for decades delayed government-aided health programs simply by labeling them "*socialized* medicine." Politicians have been against crime for centuries, but it took public-relations genius to turn it into "crime in the *streets.*"

All of these possibilities are not only unprovable, they also are quite beside the point. As Whorf warned us, the essential thing is the structure of a language —its grammar and syntax and modes of thought—and not its vocabulary, which is the least stable part of any language.

What is probably an erroneous emphasis on vocabulary has again come into vogue, this time in connection with Black Power. The year before his death, Dr. Martin Luther King called for "the reconstruction of the English language to upgrade the word black. . . . They even tell us that a white lie is better than a black lie." And indeed, the colors "black" and "white" have particular connotations for us. White is celestial, clear, pure, the skin color of the All American Girl. Black is evil, deathly, hellish.

How much truth is there in this widespread idea that race prejudice is due to the symbolism of our language? Probably none at all, for the same symbolism is found in other cultures and other language families around the world, including many in which prejudice against black skin is unknown. It occurs in Sanskrit, ancient Greek, Latin, Hebrew, Arabic, Hindi, Japanese, African languages, and probably many others. I have found it among the American Indians. The Navaho language even has *two* words for our "black"—one to indicate the blackness of things and the other for such sinister ideas as "darkness."

Would that race prejudice could be abolished by merely changing the dictionary!

The hope is that the Whorf hypothesis has brought into the open the problems inherent in language. Charles F. Hockett of Cornell, who in general has not agreed with the hypothesis, nevertheless has conceded: "Languages differ not so much as to what *can* be said in them, but rather as to what it is *relatively easy* to say in them. The history of Western logic and science constitutes not so much the story of scholars hemmed in and misled by the nature of their specific languages, as the story of a long and fairly successful struggle *against* inherited linguistic limitations. Where everyday language would not serve, special subsystems (mathematics, e.g.) were devised." The true value of Whorf's years of work with an obscure American Indian language is that he has alerted us to a problem that becomes more pressing as more people in the world communicate with each other.

Peter Farb has made the North American continent his subject—its anthropology, geology, ecology. This article is based on research for his new book, Man's Rise to Civilization as shown by the Indians of North America from Primeval Times to the Coming of the Industrial State. *It is a Book-of-the-Month Club selection.*

The View from Babel

Or: Benjamin Lee Whorf revisited.

In which we discover that the gift of languages can be a dubious blessing

On rainy evenings sometimes I wonder what it's like to be born to a single language. To speak, work, and live within the scope of this one serviceable tongue, launching into others largely in the spirit of an excursion—for pleasure perhaps? Curiosity? A school requirement? To be otherwise aware of foreign languages only in films, if at all, or strange names in newspaper headlines. To accept the polyglot world as just another geographical fact, not the ingrained and inchoate substance of whatever you eat or dream or once slid under as a child.

Rainy evenings are ideal for this sort of conjecture, maybe because they muffle the insistence of your immediate surroundings. Wet pavements look like wet pavements all the world over; it's easier then to bring together the different languages you inhabit, for their differences seem to stand equal beneath the anonymous rain.

The differences are of all kinds. Physical differences, as in a certain sound your tongue gets used to or a certain gesture that impels your hands. Mental differences, whether in your proficiency or in your associations: those subtler and more subjective contours of knowledge that come from living every day with another language. Apropos of which, there's my own dubious smattering of Spanish. It was picked up piecemeal—partly in a classroom but mainly when I married into a Spanish-speaking people—simply by learning to place everything from a political opinion to the exasperated edge of family squabbles in it. Always easy to pronounce, it now brought a pause, a rhythm, and an extravagance even

easier to assimilate. So, though I'm still not proficient in the language, it has become an irreplaceable part of my consciousness and to that extent I "know" it.

Obviously this kind of knowledge could never be allowed by any self-respecting dictionary definition. According to Webster, a bilingual is "a person using two languages habitually and with a control like that of a native speaker." By logical extension, then, a multilingual should be similarly versed in several languages. Yet the human brain, we're told, is incapable of handling more than two or three languages with any degree of perfection. Clearly there are exceptions to this rule: a linguist, for one, or a professional interpreter. Yet, however polylingual a linguist may be, even he deals usually with what one expert calls a rather "limited set of notions." The expert explains that to be "at home" in another language is much harder, for "knowing two languages perfectly means, among other things, remembering two words or phrases for every little detail of life." That in turn becomes a question of emphasis rather than efficiency, for often, depending on a bilingual's environment or personal predilection, one of his languages gains ascendancy while the other correspondingly lapses.

I can't equate my languages at all. Put them side by side and they promptly stand in a snaggle-toothed row, refusing to be bound by the same rule: one has become a tool, another its possible alternative; a third is reduced to an instinct; the fourth hovers in my head

like a tantalizing tune almost out of reach; a fifth is a backdrop to the whole lot; and so on. For, growing up in India, you become a polyglot by osmosis. Or if you don't, you should: at the last count we had seventeen major languages—each with a script and substantial literature of its own—and more than five hundred individual dialects. There's even a resigned old proverb saying "Language changes every fifteen miles," which about sums up the ensuing chaos. To complicate matters further I myself happen to come from an unusually peripatetic family, and so I needed a constant working facility with several languages at a time. In a place like New Delhi, as a result, we generally wound up speaking English to friends, Hindustani to local street vendors, Tamil to our South Indian cook, and a conglomeration of all three plus our own dialect to one another.

Trying to get a corporate professional viewpoint on what this kind of existence can do to your mind, I recently combed through libraries for every authority available—from philosophers and psychologists to linguists and educators, in turn offering meticulous surveys of school children and ethnic groups who had to contend with more than one language. In the 1920's these studies turned out to be uniformly gloomy: at worst the bilingual child was seen floundering hopelessly in the wake of his class; grown up, he could hope at best to achieve 95 per cent efficiency in two languages instead of 100 per cent in one. Then in the 1960's statistics taken at Milwaukee and Montreal made an abrupt *volte-*

By PADMA PERERA

face, announcing that bilingual school children showed "superiority in concept-formation, greater mental flexibility and a more diversified set of mental abilities than their monolingual classmates." All of which was highly edifying, but didn't begin to tap the varieties of linguistic experience I was really concerned with.

For if, as many of us have had to do, you've grown up speaking an average of four languages a day and writing an average of two, being polyglot is neither an accomplishment nor even the muddleheaded necessity it started out to be. Finally it becomes an inescapable way of seeing your world. Perceptions tend to be refracted through the prism of another language (try translating slang), especially when the change in language also implies a radical change of culture. For instance that well-known dichotomy within the Westernized Easterner—of thinking like an Occidental, feeling like an Oriental, never knowing how you will respond to a given situation—can extend to language as well. To paraphrase one astute citizen of both worlds, Han Suyin: you known sudden transpositions, baffling to yourself, in the meanings of words; you find no collateral concept in one language to explain what is clear to you in another; you attach a different significance to the same word in different cultural contexts.

Take "green" for example. In my own language the word for me is imbued with the intense life-giving color of rice fields, filling the belly and staving off death. In English it has seasonal implications (summer leaves) and overtones of ineptitude (a greenhorn, a novice; novices in the Indian languages I know aren't green, merely unripe). And after Lorca's "*verde que te quiero verde*" (green, how I love you, green), the Spanish "green" is unrivaled—even by Marvell's famous "green thought in a green shade." Translating poetry can be disastrous. I drove myself crazy one sleepless night trying to render into the Hindi language the woman "so ex-

quisitely wrought that e'en her body thought." In Hindi she wasn't and it didn't.

Hindi has other quirks. Spoken well it can sound like poetry, capable of a lilting vehemence that works perfectly for every contemporary idiocy from the mush of film songs to the tub thumping of politicians. However, Hindi has to be groomed if it's to become India's national language some day (over the dead body of several million irate non-Hindi speakers). So on the one hand it's asked to grapple with scientific jargon, and on the other it's injected with large doses of Sanskrit words to

rious and sesquipedalian process that fools no one but its perpetrators. For me, even while loving the language as I do and possibly because of some matching quirks in myself, to use it as an adult means of expression is to find suddenly that it's a gawky adolescent, all angles and elbows: try being mature, you sound bombastic; try being simple, you sound puerile.

Konkani, my own dialect, is another experience entirely. It seems to have originated, in some form, in medieval Kashmir, where it was spoken by Saraswath Brahmans before they were dispersed by Moslem invaders. I call it a dialect for want of a better word. Unlike English dialects, most of which remain recognizably English and scarcely

modify the standard tongue, Konkani is only nominally a dialect; actually it's a distinct language in itself. In fact, the last I heard, somebody was agitating for a parliamentary measure to have it decreed one of the recognized Indian languages under the constitution. At any rate, today it is spoken with extraordinary variations up and down the southwest coast—larded with Bombay's Marathi at the northern end, Kerala's Malayalam at the southern end, and Portuguese in between, around Goa.

Our particular branch of Saraswaths, which numbers about fifty thousand in all, speaks its own version of Konkani. The nucleus of the community is centered around the port of Mangalore. Others, like my family, are scattered across various parts of the country where we're monotonously accused of being northern by southerners and southern by northerners—in part because of our customs and predilections (we eat southern food but like northern music) but chiefly because of our language. We are defined by our dialect, and that remains a hybrid anomaly, occasionally given to surprises. For instance, while the rest of India is about 45 per cent literate, those who speak our version of the dialect have come up with an amazing 100 per cent literacy rate in other languages—a matter more of eccentricity than pride, really, since Konkani itself has no script. Borrow one from another language, and what you have on the page resembles nothing so much as a vast impediment of speech.

For myself, possessing a mother tongue of this sort has meant getting a unique perspective on all other languages. First of all, when you're generally preoccupied with setting things down on paper, it's a curious comfort to have recourse to a language where this is quite impossible. Perhaps in consequence, I can never forget Konkani no matter how long I am away from its source. Sometimes nasal and sometimes full of a most fetching sweetness, it wasn't the first language I learned, but it's the one that springs most quickly to my mind in moments of stress, or between sleep and waking, or to give instinctive voice to any need. "I'm hungry" or "I want to go home" are never so immediate in any other tongue. (For an image or an abstraction, on the other hand, one seeks elsewhere; watching the tender new leaves of spring, it is in English that I think, "They look like pinpoints of green light . . .") When you slide into such a dialect you also inevitably slide into its habits of thought. It makes you lazy: not surprisingly, considering that even after centuries of localization it is still too casual and rootless to have evolved its own script. Speaking Konkani is an altogether slapdash and undemanding process. The vocabulary is limited, but you don't expect it to be otherwise; and if you're at a loss for a word there's always another language close at hand from which to help yourself to a substitute. I can think of only one person —an irascible old pedant I once met— who insisted on speaking our dialect in its purest possible form, without so much as a single suffix borrowed from anywhere. After a couple of sentences he began to sound like a comic turn, and in the end he died complaining that no one ever took him seriously. Outside of this exception, there isn't a trace of self-consciousness involved in speaking our dialect. Even the inanities of baby talk come easily in Konkani. However, it does have idiosyncrasies: for example, where other languages might anthropomorphize, ours does the opposite. Every aspect of animal and vegetable life is observed in minute and loving detail and then transposed to the human condition without batting an eyelid. "Whatever you do," I remember being cautioned as a child, "do it slowly and carefully like a cockroach inserting its whisker in a hole."

On the whole, though, it's the oldest ladies in a family who use the dialect with the utmost panache, handing down a fine lunacy of proverbs and similes and admonitions you couldn't remotely begin to hear elsewhere. In no other idiom that I know are gods and demons such intimate creatures, or ordinary phrases fraught with so much implication. "Slicing a vegetable" isn't just slicing a vegetable; it is an act that, performed by a pregnant woman during an eclipse, could deform the unborn child. This is not mere overstatement or superstition but an attribute of our wholly oral tradition in which casual remarks take on the timbre and burden of inherited memory. No piece of knowledge is ever laid to rest; sooner or later some submerged wisdom or legend comes to the surface, adding to

DRAWINGS BY CHAS B SLACKMAN

the cumulative lore. Every time a clan gathers for a wedding or a festival there is sure to be one accommodating old lady tucked away in the house, who has all the time in the world to listen and tell and whose endless fund of stories is matched only by her infinite patience with children. With her stories she bequeaths her idiom—never wholly archaic and yet never wholly contemporary, either.

My brother and sister and I rediscovered this idiom whenever we visited a favorite great-uncle and two great-aunts who lived in a small South Indian town clustered untidily at the foot of a holy hill. Every day the two old ladies attended lectures on the Bhagavad-Gita, and every night they sat out on their front steps to conduct a post-mortem on what they had learned. At such times the most impressive of Sanskrit quotations could not surpass the rolling dignity of our own dialect's "howevers" and "neverthelesses," which usually flavored their disquisitions. Lying there half-asleep with our heads in their laps, we would hear those words flying back and forth above us—words we could chew like lozenges, or stretch, or spit out, or repeat over and over again in ceaseless discovery and delight, giddy as a dog chasing its own tail. We were to do this many times and in many languages across our childhood but never perhaps with such complete satisfaction.

Songs rising from carts and fields and lonely roads; the chatter of peasant women anywhere in the country when they walked past on market day, jingling their heavy silver jewelry; the patois spoken by Delhi's jaman pickers, which always sounded to me every bit as acrid and purple as the fruit they had come to gather—these were just a few of the overtones that could layer a particular language in a particular setting. Combined with a hundred other details, they gave us an evocative lore that in its own way wasn't so different from that of the old ladies in the family. Our lore was anecdotal rather than legendary, that was all; spread thinner over more languages and paced perhaps to suit a different generation. Like many others whose background made a similar patchwork, we accumulated an inevitable fund of jokes we ourselves thought hugely amusing even if no one else did, all based on the experience of more than one language. We relished the most dreadful of interlingual puns and malapropisms; or long, involved taradiddles about a misplaced housewife who bargains with local tradesmen using entire sentences uttered devastatingly in one language with the exact intonation of another; or trilingual word games and puzzles that could descend to a frenzy of cheating all around.

In all of this, how you originally met up with a language had a lot to do with how you played its games afterward. The rest of my family possessed what is called "linguistic virginity"—the power to make minds blank, linguistically speaking, to retire into the inarticulate and emerge again in a new language—so they managed to effect the smoothest of transitions everywhere we went. My own encounters with languages, however, were more reminiscent of a globe-trotting friend of mine who has a penchant for finding himself in places at the precise moment when disaster strikes: he was trapped in Mexico during one of its worst earthquakes, got stuck in a Manhattan elevator the night the power failed, and hit Japan whenever a typhoon did. So it was that I usually stumbled upon languages at an eleventh hour of crisis to discover that an entrance requirement had just been changed or a new university regulation set up. The requirement usually ceased just where my interest began, so that, plodding on from there on my own, I acquired a bumbling devotion to the tongue that was quite out of proportion to my original need. A hero of my childhood was an otherwise nondescript uncle who could, unlike myself, perform the most astounding sleights of tongue. He could put a handkerchief into his linguistic hat and take out a rabbit. He could juggle endlessly with languages, rotating four at a time in the air while I sat openmouthed wondering how long he could keep it up. The frustration that goes with such delight of course is that now I can repeat none of this in English.

For, as every translator knows, words may mean the same thing in various languages, but they seldom feel the same. Part of being polylingual is being perpetually caught in the limboes between languages—limboes not only of feeling but often of fact. You come up against that certain lack in a language, an absence of vocabulary and thought alike, when some words don't exist simply because they have no cultural *raison d'être:* no idea or experience to warrant them. Thus we hear that the first missionaries landing in the Andaman Islands, all bursting to convert the heathens, found to their stupefaction that the local tribes had no word for "God"! And thus many of us Asians still find that modern European languages often have no counterpart to those nouns with which we scrupulously identify all the relationships possible within a clan, not to mention the separate forms of address demanded by each (which sometimes leads me to suspect that my own affection for English may have sprung from sheer relief at discovering how many of my kin I could lump together under the general category of cousin).

However, on more complex levels, nothing I'd heard or read could either prepare me beforehand for all the nuances implied by this hiatus between languages, or really explain them afterward. Why did a nursery superstition like "Things happen in threes" never make one quail as did the far more ominous "*Jamais deux sans trois*"? And what incomparable grace did the simplest Greek "*kalimera*" have that our own greetings somehow never matched? The thrill of the exotic was only part of it. After all, heaven knows, there were gaps enough even in the connotations of a single word within a single language. Bertrand Russell, speaking of social and individual knowledge, remarks on how a word like "rain," for example, can have a completely different meaning for a child in the tropics as opposed to a child in a temperate climate. For me, straddling both worlds, this applied in another way: "rain" in any Indian language could resound with the immediate fury of a monsoon, whereas in English it was more malleable, accommodating everything from a drizzle to a downpour.

As long as experience molds the word and both occur in different languages across differing cultures, there can be no hard and fast formulas left. A rule of thumb in one language becomes a *non sequitur* in another. Cour-tesies grow flexible: you discover how politely you can be rude in Urdu; conversely, insolence in the Eastern world becomes candor in the West, leaving you to applaud directness in the very breath that you deplore it. Even the quality of the imagination shifts. When, in an essay he wrote, Robert Louis Stevenson described a friend wondering herself crazy over the human eyebrow, it's perfectly clear to me that she wondered in English: in at least three other languages I can think of, the process would have been not only heavy-handed but heavy-footed, too—rather like walking in glue. Then, before you know it, metaphors and imprecations change places. If an owl, so proudly stamped on an Athenian coin, is guaranteed wise in English, in Hindustani it is the ultimate epithet for stupidity. You cross such varying ranges of attitude and expression that when by chance they do transect, it is with significance to none but yourself.

Last week a friend and I were spending an evening together. It was raining outside; inside I had maundered on and on much as I have in these pages and much about the same things. Finally we drifted off into a companionable quiet, listening to the drumming on the roof, peering out through blurred windows into a light as splintered as my languages. I thought again then how their disparate elements always came together, not fused but somehow made synonymous under the common shrouding denominator of rain—how being caught between words and languages was after all as human a predicament as being caught between emotions or principles, and that acknowledging the babel inside your head was just another way of saying yes to life.

Padma Perera was born in Hejmadi, India, where she started acquiring her over-abundance of languages. Now living in New York, she is a free-lance writer and appears frequently in The New Yorker. *This is her first article for* HORIZON.

The Literary Larceny of Saint Columba

Beneath a rude arch Columba preaches to heathens in a drawing from a ninth-century Irish manuscript of his first biography.

Every night he would sneak off
in the dark to indulge
his secret lust—his lust for
copying a rare
manuscript of the Gospels

By PHYLLIS McGINLEY

Behind every myth lies a truth; beyond every legend is reality, as radiant (sometimes as chilling) as the story itself.

I am reminded of this whenever I read a bit of Saint Patrick's Day oratory or hear an Irish-American chauvinist boast the ancient glories of Holy Ireland. "Land of Saints and Scholars" runs the famous brag, and one is inclined by bored habit to put it down as defensive sloganeering.

Yet the truth and the fable go hand in hand. Little Eire was, after Cromwell, a "most distressful country" and is now merely a charming republic in the North Atlantic with a precarious balance of trade. Nonetheless in her high day the glory was genuine. For several hundred years—from the fifth century until the tenth—in that green, garrulous, rain-washed, crotchety island the twin lights of learning and Christianity burned steadily, when over Europe they had almost entirely flickered out. Actual saints and real scholars preserved a persecuted faith, a classic but perishing literature, and by their immense efforts restored both to Western Europe when the era was ripe.

"While Pope Gregory the Great was reproving a Gallic Bishop for studying Latin grammar and poetry," writes the British historian George Macaulay Trevelyan, "the Irish Christians were busy saving it for the world in their remote corner where the Papal censure was unheard."

"Remote" is the key word. Ireland, never having been conquered (or civilized) by the Roman legions, remained safely itself until the ravages of the Vikings in the ninth and tenth centuries and of the Englishman Strongbow (Richard FitzGilbert de Clare, Earl of Pembroke) in 1170 reduced it to a vassalage. And by then her wandering missionaries had done their work in Scotland, in England, on the Continent. Europe was again Christian, and knowledge had revived. The Dark Ages were over.

In one man among Ireland's heroes who thrived during the first ecstatic centuries is embodied all that is most characteristic of the Irish nature. He was Columba, also called Columkill, "The Dove of the Church."

As usual with the early saints, his life is ambered in legend. But enough facts remain to know the historical rudiments of the legend, and I tell the story as it has come down to us through Adamnan, an abbot of Iona who wrote Columba's biography a hundred years after the saint's death, through the eighth-century English historian Bede, and through tradition.

In person Columba was Irish as he was in spirit. "His eyes were the color of gray sea-water"; he was tall, fair-skinned, dark-haired, owning a voice—as one chronicler amusingly says, "so loud and melodious it could be heard a mile off." Supposedly he was a prince in his land, which ran rather to chieftains than sovereigns, for his father headed a branch of the Clan O'Neill, who were the island's most important family. Finnian of Moville was his first teacher. After Finnian had steeped him well in the classics, Columba was sent to study under "an aged bard" named Master Gemman. For despite the fact that Ireland was by the sixth century both literate and Christian, tradition dies slowly, and the bards, who had once been their country's sole historians, still possessed great power. They harped in the kings' halls and sat at the kings' tables. They presided over wars, weddings, funerals, celebrations; and at times they interpreted the laws. Columba was talented enough at versemaking to be admitted to the Bardic Order. But he opted in young manhood to become a priest and set about establishing his own churches and study centers.

However, he was yet no saint. In fact he was on his way to becoming a great sinner, and the cause of his sin was an overpowering lust for the written page.

While paying a visit to Finnian he was shown a magnificent manuscript chained to the stones of the library. It was a manuscript of the Gospels that Columba did not himself possess.

"May I copy it?" he asked; and the request seems to us perfectly reasonable. Still we cannot from our twentieth-century glut of books understand how tremendous a treasure the manuscript must have then appeared or how jealously it was guarded. At any rate, Finnian inhospitably refused.

"You may read it a thousand times, but you may not copy it," he said. "It is unique."

Columba's hold on his monastic vow of obedience was not very secure. To him Finnian must have seemed as ungracious and niggardly as he does to us. So, tempted by greed for the Word, he became a kind of thief. Night after night he crept illicitly downstairs to reproduce for himself the book that captured his imagination. When the "theft" was discovered, Finnian demanded back Columba's copy. He got nowhere, for when two obstinate Irishmen fall out, there can be no meeting of minds. Finally the case was taken to Diarmuid, the High King, for his arbitration. Then came the famous decision that has for years so diverted historians.

"Both manuscripts belong to Finnian," said Diarmuid. "I follow the Law. To every cow its calf and to every book its son-book."

Wild with disappointment, Columba rushed back not to his monastery but to the headquarters of his clan.

"Avenge me this injustice," he cried to the O'Neills.

Probably, since they were a lively lot, they enjoyed the excuse for a scrimmage. But what followed was not a local dustup but a genuine battle in which, says the tale, three thousand men were slain. The story goes on to describe Columba's belated horror when he saw the bodies of the fallen and realized he was responsible for their deaths.

It was then that he swore his eternal vow.

"I have committed a crime against God and Ireland. God I will pray to for the rest of my life. Also for the rest of my life I promise never again to look upon Irish shores."

So he embarked in his currach with twelve companions—all relatives—and sailed across wild waters until Ireland disappeared. When even on a clear day he could no longer make out its beloved shape, he stopped at an island and there began to build a chapel.

The island was Iona, in the Hebrides off the coast of Scotland. And the monastery he finally founded there was to be the longest-lasting and the most influential of all the Celtic abbeys. From that base he converted the pagan Scottish people of the mainland, as well as the islanders. From it, too, went forth the most successful of the pioneering monks into Britain. And also there Columba tamed his own defiant spirit into a gentleness still lauded by his countrymen. He taught scholars. He worked in the fields with his monks and protected the beasts and wild fowl, which, the legend tells, flocked about him. It is said that when he was dying even his old horse shed tears of sorrow.

He left Iona only once. In his sole journey back to the Ireland he had forsworn he did not, however, break his vow. He kept his word by a ruse worthy of wily Odysseus.

In his absence the bards had become national nuisances. Brimming over with pride of office, they had begun to drive hard bargains for their services. They meddled with politics, asked enormous prizes for presiding over a victory or a marriage, and in

This embellished Latin script is a piece of the earliest known manuscript produced in the British Isles. It is from the famous Cathrach, *or "battle psalter," and it may well be inscribed in the hand of Saint Columba.*

general paraded their power like officials—and poets—in every generation. The always-prickly natives rose against them. At Tara, the regal hill fortress, they besought the king to put a stop to bardic misconduct.

The current occupant of the High Seat must have been a man as impulsive as the young Columba. Instead of merely reproving the bards, the king decided to exile them. Terrified by the sentence, the bards could think of nothing to do except enlist Columba on their side.

"You are one of us," they told him by messenger. "Without you we perish."

Then came the problem. The saint in his tolerant solitude could realize better than his exploited countrymen how Ireland would miss its praisers. Besides, he loved a well-turned verse. But how could he "look again on Ireland's shores" when he had made that solemn pledge?

Well, he could go without looking, could travel blindfolded to court. And that, of course, is what he did.

Once at Tara he spoke with such eloquence to the gathering that they changed their stubborn minds.

"Meddlers and muddlers these bards may be," he reminded them. "But without their songs, who will remember your glories? Who will harp the tales of your wars, the beauty of your women? You will lose your history."

So the poets were allowed to stay, and Columba went back to Iona, blindfolded as he had left it, to live out his days in peaceful, God-fearing austerity.

When Ireland's freedom and isolation were finally shattered, Iona's monastery, like those on the mainland, was destroyed by steel and flame. Of all that passionate industry—the splendor of manuscripts lovingly illuminated, the artistry, the composing—few relics of stature remain. One of them sits now in the library of Dublin's Trinity College. There one can gape at it under its protective glass, stare at its pages, turned one at a time and once a day. It is the superb Book of Kells, a large manuscript of the Gospels believed to date from the eighth or early ninth century, and ranks among the most beautiful manuscripts in the world. It was discovered in County Meath near the ruins of what was probably one of Columba's own early foundations.

Yet, in spite of the destruction, something more important than a few books has been salvaged from the rubble of a quirky civilization. We have the learning those early saints and scholars preserved for us, the impact of their religious fervor. And we have the memory of their myth-encrusted lives. Forever about them glimmers (to quote once more from Trevelyan) "the freshness and the light of the dawn."

For five years Phyllis McGinley, who won the 1961 Pulitzer Prize for Poetry, has been working on a book about "various aspects of sanctity." Her tentative title is Saint Watching, *and she describes her book, which will include this essay, as "part history, part prejudice."*

Render unto Cedar

The totem poles of the Pacific coast are vanishing
into the earth. "It is," says our author,
"an art that knew how to live, and now it knows how to die."

The last totem poles stand on deserted beaches at the edge of cedar forests, gazing out to sea as if they were watching for the wakes of dolphins and killer whales. Only a very few are left now, among the hundreds of wooded islands that dot the Pacific coast from Nootka, on Vancouver Island, to Yakutat Bay, Alaska—a thousand miles of indescribably jagged coastline, where snow-capped mountains plunge into a sea perpetually warmed by the Japan Current.

Until the turn of the century many of the Indian villages in this region had veritable forests of totem poles on their landing beaches: in Tuxekan, for example, a visitor in 1916 counted one hundred and twenty-five of them. But the missionaries were opposed to them, not knowing or caring that they were heraldic crests and images of memory rather than heathen idols. In a way their attitude is understandable. If you have once seen some of these great sculptures swaying in the wind, and felt the power of their stare, you no longer wonder why a missionary could not tolerate having them forever peering over his shoulder.

After the missionaries came the anthropologists and museum curators to do some more cutting down, though from other motives. They have gone into the most remote and nearly inaccessible places, such as Anthony Island, to put the last salvageable poles under protective custody. As a result,

Above, a tree grows from the head of a Kwakiutl pole on Turner Island, British Columbia. Opposite, like a curtain drawing shut, vines close over the face of a fallen totem pole in Kwakiutl cemetery.

the likeliest place to find a proper totem pole nowadays is at some institution of higher collecting like the University of British Columbia at Vancouver, the Museum of Natural History in New York, or the British Museum in London, which has a marble staircase winding around a three-story Haida pole from the Queen Charlotte Islands, perhaps the finest in existence.

The coast as a whole has been just about stripped of its primitive art in any case. For the past twenty years or so, led first by the French surrealist poet André Breton and then by Nelson Rockefeller, the great northwest-coast art rush has been on at the galleries and auction houses: a Tlingit dance mask that might have brought seventy-five dollars in 1945 was worth ten times that in 1955 and is now almost unobtainable at any price. Whatever was left on the coast after a century and a half of missionizing and souvenir hunting has been sluiced down to the big city dealers. Portable items were the first to go, but lately even ten-ton packages are being shipped out. I remember an immense, raven-beaked skeleton of a Kwakiutl long house that stood at Village Island, British Columbia, until two years ago; then it was loaded onto a raft and floated down to a collector in Tacoma (at a price, the neighbors claim, of ten thousand dollars).

Ironically enough, most of this art was originally made for the express purpose of being given away, since the way to acquire status in this part of the world, in the old days, was to amass a hoard of beautiful things and then hand them over to other people at one of the great belching, brawling potlatch banquets. This was not quite as selfless as it sounds. The gift giving

By FREDERIC V. GRUNFELD

became compulsive when potlatching replaced tribal warfare as a way of settling disputes and rival chiefs were forced to outshine each other in periodic orgies of largesse.

It was that rare and curious phenomenon, a materialist but nonacquisitive society. The artists it produced were probably the greatest wood sculptors of all time and the most gifted depictors of the face. Nothing else in the realm of wood sculpture can quite compare with the magnificent classicism of these masks and totems: the Congo carvers, though no less imaginative, tend to be far more nervous and arbitrary in their forms, while the Gothic sculptors of Europe could muster none of the magic powers of the totem—their scale is small and hedged about with inhibitions, as the pear tree is to the giant cedar.

This is an art of faces and eyes that goes far beyond the Greek ideal of *physeōs mimēsis*—the imitation of nature—which has hamstrung the European tradition for two thousand years. Though undeterred by the tyranny of appearances, even the most abstract of the totem faces are somehow remarkably alive. Perhaps the head-hunting tendencies along the coast had something to do with giving the Indian carvers this superb appreciation of what goes on above the neck. We know from other parts of the world that hunters are the keenest observers and thus potentially the best artists; certainly there have never been more vivid animal-paintings than those of the sorcerer-hunters of Lascaux. The sculptors of the northwest coast, oddly enough, prized human faces and animal heads but cared nothing at all for the body. At best they simply dissected it, and they could pass with perfect equanimity (and without a break in line) from showing us the outside of a whale—fins, eyes, mouth, tail—to the inside, with a cross section of the bone structure and a catalogue of the contents of the stomach.

Having invented this kind of X-ray

A last stand of totems in a Kwakiutl cemetery

Haida warrior's face

Clothesline, Village Island

Guilford Island: grimace in the grass

Kwakiutl grave marker

Haida pole, Skidegate Mission

vision, it was only natural that they should return again and again to the symbolism of the all-seeing eye. It dominates the whole of the northwest-coast sculpture—Haida, Nootka, or Kwakiutl; Tsimshian, Bella Coola, or Tlingit. Before the white man came, every implement these Indians used bore the eyes and faces of art: their weapons, blankets, dance rattles, harpoons, dishes, and "soul catchers," or spirit bottles. The forms and patterns are capable of being adapted to innumerable practical (and impractical) shapes. A totem design may be magnified to cover the side of a house; it can be bent around corners to decorate the four sides of a storage box; can be cut in intaglio into a horn spoon, woven into a robe, or hammered onto the handle of a knife.

Since the designs all told their stories, the tools they ornamented became charged with symbolic meaning. While it lasted, it must have been a society in which (strange as it may sound to us, living in the age of the rusty tin can) *everything had style.* The high point of this organic art was the totem pole, the life-affirming figure that proclaimed man's place in this landscape. Erected with great effort and potlatch ceremonial, these artificial trees staked out his territory among the living cedars. They spelled out the owner's lineage, like a European coat of arms, or served as *aides-mémoire* to the storyteller. Most of the stories involved the various animals from whom the owners were symbolically descended, like the one about the raven and the grizzly bear going fishing:

Raven caught many halibut, but Bear caught nothing. Bear asked Raven what kind of bait he was using. Raven mumbled something Bear did not understand and went on fishing. He again asked Raven what kind of bait he used, and Raven finally told him to cut a piece of meat off of himself if he wanted to catch halibut. Bear protested, but Raven told him his wife would be very angry if he came home without any halibut. Then he began to taunt Bear and call him a coward because he was afraid to cut a piece of meat from himself for bait. Raven wanted to kill Bear anyway because he did not want to share his catch with him. Finally Bear did as Raven directed and bled to death . . .

All the participants in such a tale—including the cormorant who assists Raven and the halibut they catch—will be shown as interlocking figures on the pole. Today, of course, only a few very old people can remember the tales, and the handful of carvers still active in the area have lost the art of interpreting them.

The last surviving poles usually stand in deserted villages, where the forest is slowly reclaiming its own. Often the tops are broken off and only the lower halves remain. Once a pole falls to the ground it soon becomes enveloped in raspberry bushes. But yellow cedar does not capitulate so quickly, even when it is half buried in the earth. The poles lie on the ground for many years, grass growing from their nostrils, their backs partly decayed but their animal faces still formidable, the bears' teeth ready to bite. The cedar forest begins just beyond them: gnarled roots and giant trunks that rise up for a hundred feet. Beneath them lie other immense trunks felled by natural infirmities years before. There is scarcely any underbrush, and the ground, springy to the step, is carpeted with needles. The shapes of the dead trees, their broken branches covered with moss, bear an uncanny resemblance to the fallen totems: where does this art leave off and the environment begin?

Here, too, are mounds of burial boxes, stacked up like so many drawers taken from a dresser, with only a shingle roof to ward off the rain. Sometimes a wooden fence has been built around the pile like a parody of a New England churchyard. But the roof has collapsed, the contents of the coffins have spilled out, so that you see pieces of half-mummified limbs— feet, generally, with chalk-white toenails, or fairly lifelike hands, apparently wrapped in some sort of linen —scattered among clean-picked bones and skulls. Rib cage and backbone may still be together in a recognizable relationship, but more often the skeleton is just a pile of blanched pick-up sticks. The deceased were sent on to the next world in the fetal position. They were wrapped in red trade blankets (adorned, of course, with white-shell button designs) that are now in the last stages of decay, so that some skulls seem to be covered with fresh blood—dye from the blanket moldering in the rain. Other burial boxes are so old they contain nothing but humus, and already there are new bushes and cedar saplings growing out of them, just as they sprout from the broken heads of totems.

Which suggests to me that there is, perhaps, another lesson to be learned from these cedar sculptures, a lesson that has less to do with forms than with the dissolution of forms and the mortality of art. Much of our Western art, and Asian art as well, represents an attempt to stay the fell hand of the executioner, time and decay: from the days of the Pharaohs onward we have built monuments in stone and bronze so that we could extend our sway and power beyond the grave. "Great art endures," we say confidently, and worry when the paint flakes off the *Last Supper.* But the cedar figures on the totem poles abide by the timetable of the forest. These eyes, which see so profoundly beyond the surface of things, also gaze into the essential nature of this physical earth and the cycle of renewal that is necessary to it. It is an art that knew how to live, and now it knows how to die.

An expert on primitive art, Frederic V. Grunfeld has several times journeyed with his wife, photographer Toby Molenaar, to the shores of British Columbia and Alaska. Many of her photographs were taken on a trip for the Riveredge Foundation, Calgary.

Kitwancool, British Columbia: soon only the shacks will re

Napoleon Slept Here

After his daring escape from Elba, the Emperor marched from Golfe-Juan to Paris. If he had stopped at every inn that claims him along the way, he would have been late for Waterloo

Golfe-Juan. From the café of the snug little Hôtel Napoléon I could see the hexagonal blue mosaic plaque sunk in the quay opposite, and when I had finished breakfast, I crossed the boulevard through the chaos of summer Riviera traffic. The plaque, topped by the imperial eagle, bore the inscription "Here Napoleon landed in 1815."

I have been a Bonaparte buff since adolescence, and as I contemplated the tourist-choked site, fragments of his last great adventure before Waterloo flashed through my mind. . . . The escape from Elba on February 26 with barely a thousand men aboard the brig *l'Inconstant* and six smaller craft. Napoleon on deck, paunchy and sallow in middle age, a tricolor cockade sewn to his bicorn hat, distributing to his officers the proclamation secretly printed in exile: "Comrades, trample the white cockade underfoot. It is the emblem of shame." Chivvying his seasick treas-

On the snow-covered field of Laffrey, Napoleon rides eternally on his charger Tauris. On just such a bitter March day in 1815 the Royalist garrison deserted to the Emperor, opening the way to Paris.

urer, Baron Peyrusse: "Come, monsieur, a little Seine water will cure you." So calmly confident on the eve of landing ("I will reach Paris without firing a shot") that he played chess with his faithful General Bertrand. The midday landing, observed but unopposed by the dumbstruck townsfolk. The long march north. Louis XVIII fleeing, Napoleon's triumphal re-entry into the Tuileries within three weeks after his gamble had begun on that lonely beach.

I asked the owner of the Hôtel Napoléon whether the name of his establishment implied any historical associations. "Alas, none," he said. "The tourists are always disappointed. But I refuse to hoodwink the public like certain colleagues of mine I could mention. If Napoleon slept in all the hotels around here and ate in all the restaurants people claim he did, he would never have got to Paris. *C'est pour rigoler.* Now, if the real thing interests you . . . ?" I assured him it did, passionately. "Then you should pay a visit to an old gentleman who lives quite close." On the back of a bar tab the innkeeper scribbled the name, Félix Cevoules-Anglès, and the address, a farm off the coast highway.

I was distracted en route by a bust of Napoleon perched atop a stele towering beside the highway. It

marked the spot where the landing force regrouped for the push to Paris. Across the highway stood a *bistro* describing itself as "Auberge de l'Empereur Napoléon I, En 1815 Auberge de la Minute." A wooden menu-holder in the shape of a Napoleonic grenadier advertised "*Steack pommes frites salade 6 frs. Service 12%.*" I entered. Beneath a pink neon Napoleon sign that flashed on and off like a firefly a barmaid was serving *pastis* to a gnomish woman. Napoleonana festooned the walls—chromos depicting the landing, facsimiles of proclamations ("Soldiers! We have not been defeated . . ."), commemorative plaques ("The great Napoleon rested here. Come, wayfarer, drink and honor his name"). When I asked for the owner, the little woman spun around and scrutinized me for a moment in bleak silence. She wore a man's felt hat with the brim pulled down over her ears. A raveled sweater reached to her knees. "You desire?" she said at length.

I confessed to a curiosity about the history of the place. Her face lit up as brightly as the pink sign. "My family has owned it for generations. I am Madame Louisa Hauser, née Letendard. We make our own special orange marmalade, retaining the whole orange. The *patronne* at the time of the landing, when it was l'Auberge de la

By JOHN KOBLER

Photographed for Horizon *by* ROBERT DESCHARNES

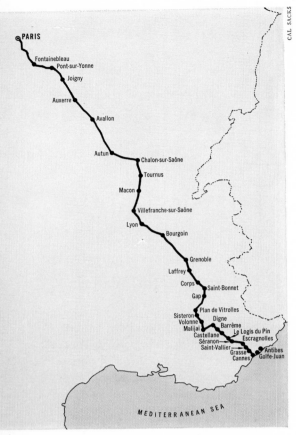

Although Napoleon's route from Golfe-Juan to Paris led through some of the most rugged country in France, he averaged an amazing twenty-eight miles a day.

Minute, was my great-grandmother, Madame Fortune. He sat in this very room and mapped his campaign. Photography didn't exist in those days, you understand, but Napoleon III, he had a photo taken and he signed it as authentic. No, I regret, impossible to show it to you today. I keep it at the bank and I'm too busy to fetch it. Do you know why Napoleon's statue out there is staring so angrily toward Antibes? Because the *Antibois* wouldn't follow him. They were traitors. Not like us folk here. Marie, a *pastis* . . ."

I wanted to believe every word the little woman uttered. But according to some of the accounts I later consulted, the original Auberge de la Minute had burned down years ago.

More tangible evidence of the Emperor's passage awaited me at the home of Monsieur Cevoules-Anglès. A tall,

spare man in his seventies, horticulturist, antiquary, and writer of television comedies, he received me in a study full of Napoleonic memorabilia. The adjoining land, he related, as he unstopped a decanter of Chartreuse, was farmed in 1815 by his great-grandfather, Jerôme Jourdan, a fervent Bonapartist. Before disembarking on March 1, Napoleon put ashore a detachment of grenadiers with orders to proceed to Antibes, about a mile distant, and win over the Royalist garrison there. Pending the outcome, he accepted Jourdan's offer of shelter. The air was bitter cold, and snow covered the foothills above the coast.

"As my grandmother used to tell me the story," my host recalled, "a badly smoking fireplace drove Napoleon out of the house. So the family moved every seat they owned to the olive orchard. There, under a giant olive tree, Napoleon shared a banquette with his aide-de-camp, General Drouot." He paused for dramatic effect. "You, my friend, are sitting on that banquette." I rose to admire the relic, a massive mahogany Empire piece with curling sides and no back. "While warming himself with wine made from our own grapes Napoleon noticed that Madame Jourdan was *enceinte*. He congratulated her, predicted a son, and proposed himself as godfather on the condition that she promise him a future grenadier for his guard of honor. As it turned out, she bore a daughter—my grandmother's sister."

Napoleon waited until late at night, my host continued. A Royalist deserter from Antibes finally reported that the garrison, far from defecting, had imprisoned the entire detachment of grenadiers. Napoleon decided to press forward without them before word of the capture spread and encouraged others to oppose him. Of the possible routes north he chose the most arduous, via Grenoble, along twisting rocky mountain paths; he believed Bourbon loyalties to be weakest in that direction. "They set

out for Cannes toward midnight. By the end of the next day, they had marched almost sixty kilometers, having passed through Grasse, Saint-Vallier, and Escragnolles to Séranon. One still finds in those places the great-grandchildren of people who saw the Emperor, talked with him, and helped him, and some of them have family heirlooms to prove it."

It sounded too good to pass up. I had three weeks of vacation left, the same length of time it took Napoleon to reach Paris. He traveled the 555-mile journey on foot, by coach, or astride his silver-gray stallion, Tauris, depending on the condition of the terrain. I had a four-cylinder Peugeot.

Cannes. I parked alongside the church of Notre Dame de Bon Voyage, which in Napoleon's day stood isolated amid sand dunes, to read an inscription identifying the site as his bivouac during the early morning of March 2. At his approach the *Cannais*, then totaling three thousand and predominantly pro-Bourbon, cowered behind closed shutters; but they emerged when the soldiers halted beyond firing range, obeying Napoleon's order not to "alarm the people." The entire population crowded around the legendary figure, impelled more by curiosity than sympathy. A butcher—so a local historian related the incident to me—nearly ended Napoleon's career then and there. He aimed a musket at the Emperor's head, but a companion, fearing a general massacre, knocked the weapon out of his hand. The mayor of Cannes stifled his Bourbon allegiance long enough to sell the invaders rations and mules and horses, provided that they advance no farther into the town. Baron Peyrusse paid him out of the two million francs' worth of gold transported aboard *l'Inconstant*, while Napoleon sat shivering before a campfire. At dawn they began the steep climb into the hills.

Grasse. The municipal council of this aromatic community, whose chief occupation then as now was distilling perfume, considered arming the populace but decided otherwise upon discovering that their entire armament amounted to thirty rusty rifles. The six thousand inhabitants, moreover, included a good many Bonapartists. They flocked to the plateau of Roquevignon, on the outskirts of the town ("Here sat Napoleon, March 2, 1815," states a marker set in a cypress grove), bringing food and drink for the troops and garlands of violets for Napoleon. The violets, a local official explained to me, held a special meaning. "The year before, when Napoleon sailed into exile from Fréjus, it was springtime, and the violets were in full bloom. He promised his partisans, 'You shall see me when the violets bloom again.' And so it was." Hence, one of Napoleon's numerous sobriquets—"Le Père-la-Violette."

As Le Père-la-Violette squatted on a pile of sacking, picking at a roast chicken, a blind veteran of the early campaigns tottered toward him, groping for his hand. Napoleon embraced him. Then for the first time since he had landed he heard Frenchmen cry, *"Vive l'Empereur!"*

Since no vehicle could mount the narrow, rutted footpath winding north from Grasse, Napoleon abandoned his artillery, which consisted of only four cannon, and had the gold transferred from coach to muleback. A tanner named Isnard joined the expedition.

Saint-Vallier-de-Thiey.

Population: 429. The aged but spry mayor, Nicolas Lombard, is a lateral descendant of Chautard, the deputy mayor who greeted Napoleon; his superior had fled rather than commit himself politically. "What were the politics of the majority?" I asked the mayor. "Opportunism," he replied.

The corpulent war lord arrived considerably shaken. Slogging through snowy mountain passes, with a stick for support, he had taken some nasty spills. One of the gold-laden mules tumbled over a precipice. As I strolled

with the mayor through the tiny village square, dominated by a statue of Napoleon, he remembered from his youth an old farmer who swore he knew where the mule had landed. "He searched for the treasure to his dying day, but he never found a louis."

Napoleon sank down on a stone bench that encircled a huge elm. "A storm destroyed the elm," said the mayor, "and we replaced it with the statue. The original bench we moved to the other elm, over there." An innkeeper named Réal, he recounted, proffered the weary Napoleon a platter of refreshments, but Napoleon, ever alert to the possibility of being poisoned, turned his back. "Fill a glass," General Bertrand ordered the innkeeper, "and drink." When he complied, Napoleon took the glass and drained it. Aflame with imperial passion, Réal thereafter called his inn Hôtel des Princes.

The mayor also told me the story about the eggs. Later that afternoon, it seems, Napoleon ate two. The peasant woman who supplied them charged him one hundred *écus*, roughly three times the normal price. *"Bon Dieu!"* exclaimed Napoleon, "eggs must be scarce around here." "No, Sire," she rejoined, "emperors are."

Escragnolles.

A name to conjure with in this ancient hamlet is Mireur. General François Mireur, as the plaque at the door of his native house sets forth, was a Napoleonic stalwart killed in action during the Egyptian campaign of 1798. "France is indebted to him for having adopted the Marseillaise as her national anthem." Napoleon, whom no politician ever surpassed as a crowd-pleaser, hastened to salute the dead hero's mother and awarded her five hundred francs. The affecting scene unfolded in what is now the Auberge Napoléon, under the ownership of one Adolphe Glise, who served me lukewarm Coca-Cola.

Of Escragnolles's present population (180) the only bearer of the illustrious name is the postman, Raymond Mi-

"Vive l'Empereur," *shouted the citizenry as Napoleon (above, under eagle) and his grenadiers disembarked at Golfe-Juan.*

Having dispatched some officers to Antibes, Napoleon accepted the hospitality of one Farmer Jourdan and sat down on this bench to await the return of his men.

Upon learning that his delegation had been imprisoned by the Antibois, *he set off toward Cannes and dined beside a campfire. Above, he is seated at the table.*

The Auberge Napoléon, now guarded by a wooden grenadier, was where Napoleon stopped to map his campaign for the march north—so the present owner says.

reur, a small, shy bachelor of thirty-five who makes his rounds in a yellow Renault station wagon. When I finally tracked him down, he proved too laconic for sustained conversation.

Séranon. Dismay overwhelms the Napoleonophile who tarries here, for what traces remain of the Emperor's passage have been allowed to fall into decay. Napoleon spent the night of March 2 at the Château de Brondet, the rustic retreat of the Marquis de Gourdon, mayor of Grasse. ("Château" is hyperbolic; old photographs show a plain farmhouse.) With difficulty I persuaded Séranon's Mayor Chiris to guide me to it. A gruff, stolid cattle breeder reluctant to leave his herd, he clearly felt he was humoring a monomaniac.

A walk through a grainfield brought us to an olive grove. There I beheld all that was left of the Château de Brondet—a clutter of toppled masonry and rotting beams overgrown with weeds. "What happened?" I asked. Chiris shrugged. "Neglect. I saw it standing in one piece before the First World War. Some Belgians bought the property, planning to make a *camping* of it, but the money ran out." He poked at a brick with the toe of his boot. "Napoleon slept on the ground floor, right about here, in an armchair, without undressing. My

son-in-law has the chair, Lord knows where, also a table Napoleon used. A legacy. The Marquis de Gourdon left the château and its contents to the curé Rebuffel. The curé left them to his cousin Philomène, a very pious maiden lady. She left them to her nephew, Léon Rebuffel, who left them to his son Emile, who married my daughter Augusta. Everything has disappeared except the chair and table." He chuckled at my eagerness. "I suppose you want to see them."

We trudged back across the field to a ramshackle barn. A stout, middle-aged woman sat in the doorway plucking a chicken. "My daughter Augusta," said the mayor, and with an air of tolerant amusement asked her to satisfy my curiosity. Leading me inside the barn, she fumbled under a pile of straw and farm debris. Presently she dragged out a walnut refectory table with spiraling legs, then a straight-backed armchair. The table drawer was missing and one of the legs broken. A last strand of green brocade upholstery hung from the chair. "A pity not to restore them," I ventured. "Ah, monsieur," said Augusta, "we have so many other tasks."

Le Logis du Pin. I lunched at the Auberge du Logis du Pin, among the oldest inns in France. So did Napoleon, on a bowl of bouillon.

By my bedside lamp that night I read the traditional account of how some brigands nearby murdered the two grenadiers guarding Napoleon's gold and emptied a chestful of it. Years later, the old-timers insist, during the construction of National Route 85, workmen unearthed two skeletons lying beside a shattered chest stamped with the imperial eagle.

Castellane. Napoleon's swift forced marches, outracing communications, had so far found no town prepared to resist him. Though he expected pursuing Royalist cavalry to harass him from the rear, no attack developed. (Not until four days after the landing

did word of his escape reach King Louis, who received it with fatuous unconcern, so sure was he that loyal subjects would stop the invader. "Not anxiety, but gout troubles me," he said.) To the blare of martial music, Napoleon rode through the town on Tauris. Sullen glances followed him, but nobody raised a hostile hand. A polite appeal to the subprefect procured Napoleon five thousand rations of bread, meat, and wine. In the subprefecture he ate a meal prepared under the vigilant eyes of two officers.

Castellane slumbers in the shadow of an immense bread-loaf rock surmounted by a statue of the Virgin Mary. The town has changed little since Napoleon's time. Recently the old subprefecture building, with its plaque commemorating the imperial meal, was converted into a family vacation hostel under the auspices of Monaco. Princess Grace herself presided at the inaugural ceremony.

Barrême. From the semicircular stone stoop to the floral wallpaper in the second-story alcove, the tall, narrow house stands much as it was when Monsieur Tartanson, the justice of the peace, enthusiastically welcomed Napoleon. The magistrate's ardor reflected the almost unanimous local sentiment, a heartening contrast to the exile's previous receptions. When Napoleon attempted to remunerate him for his bounty, which included a dinner of lentil soup, omelette, codfish, roast kid, and fruit (all dutifully tasted first by an officer), M. Tartanson protested, "I am not an innkeeper, I submit no bills."

The present tenant, the Widow Cazzola, a retired nurse, was redecorating the place when I pulled the bell chain. She was delighted to show me the alcove in which Napoleon spent the night. It appears to be just wide enough to accommodate a man

Leaving Saint-Vallier-du-Thiey, the Emperor set out upon the rocky path toward Escragnolles and the long Alpine climb.

In this alcove in a private home in Barrême, Napoleon set up his army cot and stayed the night. The dressing table is more than likely post-Napoleonic.

of his stature. "He had his own army cot brought in," she told me. "A farmer's wife came with two eggs—but I see you know the story.

Digne. The Tartanson line eventually split into two branches, one moving to Avignon, the other here. The present head of the Digne branch, Charles Tartanson, is the town's leading lawyer, a figure of seignorial dignity. In his study, opening on a walled rose garden, he seated me in a Louis XV armchair with claw feet. "It came from my great-great-grandfather's house in Barrême," he said. "Napoleon sat where you are sitting. Note the scars on the arms. He had a nervous habit when worried—and, *mon Dieu!* there was a lot to worry him—of jabbing at the arms of his chair with his penknife."

Napoleon left behind several souvenirs at the Tartanson house, among them his monogrammed bed sheets and a silver coffee service. "What he didn't leave, we took. My brother in Avignon has the sheets."

Malijai. Toward dusk on March 4, the Royalist Marquis Edouard Noguier de

Malijai returned from a hunting trip to find his château overrun by Napoleon's men. In the courtyard soldiers were burning a whole winter's provision of firewood. Mattresses clogged the halls and corridors. Napoleon had installed himself in a bedroom at the head of the main staircase. "You will have some work to do," he said, and demanded vast quantities of rations.

The Emperor passed a sleepless and anxious night by a marble fireplace. Recruits were still lacking. How long would it be before the enemy overtook him, forcing him to stand and fight? How would he cross the Durance River into Sisteron, tomorrow's objective, if the garrison there blew up the bridge? He crumpled the rough draft of a proclamation and hurled it into the grate. (Salvaged by the marquis, the charred manuscript has been preserved by his heirs.) But the great gambler's luck held. A messenger brought cheering news from General Cambronne (beloved by French schoolboys for the five-letter word he uttered in defiance of the British at Waterloo), whom Napoleon had sent ahead with an advance guard to reconnoiter. They had crossed the bridge unchallenged and were established inside the town.

Between the two World Wars the Pechiney chemical works acquired the Château de Malijai and converted one wing into apartments for its personnel. A sign outside the gates says that Napoleon camped on the grounds, a misstatement calculated to sidetrack souvenir hunters. Droves of them have already stripped the interior of practically everything removable, down to the upholstery nails in Napoleon's fireside chair. His quarters are shared today by a Pechiney foreman and his wife. Nothing could induce them to admit me. I had to content myself with the Marquis de Malijai's memoir of the unwelcome visit. "At six o'clock in the morning [it concluded] he descended the stairs as fast as he climbed them the preceding evening.

He hesitated a moment in the doorway and seemed extremely astonished to see all the inhabitants of the village assembled before the château in profound silence. . . . He apparently expected me to go up to him; I didn't budge. He recovered his composure, mounted his horse, and departed for Sisteron."

Volonne. There is no more spectacular drive in France than the chain of modern highways designated as the Route Napoléon. Coiling past snow-capped Alpine peaks, diamantine streams tumbling through depthless gorges, soaring pine forests, and green and golden plains rolling away to the horizon, the road is here and there flanked by stanchions bearing a bronze eagle—an allusion to Napoleon's pledge: "The Eagle shall fly from steeple to steeple to the spires of Notre Dame." But the Route Napoléon only approximates the course he really followed. The few stretches extant of the latter are mostly impassable by car and a formidable challenge to hikers. I marveled at the stamina of Napoleon's foot soldiers, who averaged twenty-five miles a day.

One fragment of the old route that my Peugeot did manage to negotiate borders the Durance River from Volonne to Sisteron. Bumping over it, I came to a cryptic epigraph, presumably in Provençal: *"Eishi Lou 5 de Mars 1815 N. Ier P.P."* As I pondered the meaning, a towheaded rustic driving a donkey cart pulled up and with a grin enlightened me. "It is murmured around the countryside that the Emperor was observed to urinate on this spot." In ordinary French, *"Napoléon passa et pissa."*

Sisteron. Controversy still occasionally arises among *Sisteronais* over their forefathers' failure to stop Napoleon. Some blame the mayor, Joseph Laurent de Gombert. A handful of militia, they argue, manning the guns of the lofty hilltop citadel that commands the approaches to the town, could have blasted Cambronne's cavalry off the landscape. A few kegs of gunpowder could have demolished the bridge. Pierre de Gombert, a lawyer and gentleman dairy farmer who produces yoghurt on his 625-acre domain, told me in defense of his great-great-grandfather, "No stauncher Royalist ever breathed, but what could he do? He was overruled by higher authorities. The military governor of the department had given the inexplicable order to evacuate all munitions so that they wouldn't fall into enemy hands. He may have been a secret Bonaparte sympathizer. Even then my ancestor tried to organize resistance, but the citizenry was too terrified. Consider, please, that the town council later exonerated him."

After an *apéritif* in his manor house, which dates from the early fifteenth century, M. de Gombert accompanied me to the home of a Madame Lagarde, originally the Auberge du Bras d'Or, where Napoleon ate *canard aux olives* for lunch. From the windows I gazed, bemused, as no doubt he did, at the citadel under whose silent guns he rode and at the bridge that was never blown up. "The Government put up a plaque," said Madame Lagarde, "but I took it down. It attracted too many tourists."

Plan de Vitrolles. Vicomte René d'Arnauld de Vitrolles, a retired air force general, and his wife exemplify the conciliation of once fiercely hostile factions. His great-great-grandfather, Baron Eugène de Vitrolles, helped draft Louis XVIII's constitution, served as his secretary of state, and up to the last moment struggled to thwart the "usurper." The viscountess descends from Napoleon's brother, Lucien Bonaparte. Relics of the epoch, handed down by both families, throng the majestic eighteenth-century Château de Vitrolles, which looms some two thousand feet above the site of the posthouse where Napoleon paused. A local farm boy who saw him there lived to describe him to the viscount's

father as "a fat ugly little man."

"He refused to set foot here," the viscount told me. "He sat straddling a chair in front of the posthouse, glowering at us and muttering, 'That's my worst enemy.' Actually, the baron was in Paris, working against him."

Gap. In a bedroom of the old Hôtel Marchand (not the latter-day Hôtel Napoléon, as the unwary might assume) Napoleon fired the only shot of the campaign. His target was an accretion of soot blocking the chimney, and the bullet neatly dislodged it. The Alpine provinces had proved largely pro-Bonaparte, and at last he found volunteers; he entered Gap with four times as many troops as had left Elba.

A tearoom and pastry shop, L'Halte Napoléon, now occupies the ground floor of the defunct Hôtel Marchand. It is a small gem of Empire reproduction, the burnished oak paneling ornamented with bronze scrollwork, the curvilinear stools upholstered in red-and-white-striped silk. The proprietor, Jean Pascal, a master chef, has also created a diversity of desserts evoking the imperial era, such as *les Walewskas* (named after Napoleon's Polish mistress)—a chocolate shell full of Cointreau—and *les Grognards* ("the grumblers," as his old campaigners were called)—almond cakes. I chose a slice of *Madame Sans Gêne* (the sobriquet of an uninhibited washerwoman who married one of Napoleon's marshals)—a wildly caloric chocolate and praline cake.

"Tell me," said M. Pascal, as I savored the ambrosia, "do you think people will remember de Gaulle a hundred and fifty years from now?" I said I felt sure they would. He scowled. "I am no admirer."

Saint-Bonnet. The eagle spreads his wings on a granite shaft overlooking the sultry Champsaur valley. A plaque affixed to the hotel across the road proclaims: "Here Napoleon was hailed by the peasants of Champsaur and declined their offer to join his army."

Napoleon threw some scribbled notes into the fireplace above in the château of the Marquis de Malijai, who quickwittedly saved the papers as an heirloom.

Though the hotel, l'Halte de l'Empereur, opened its doors only a few months before I dropped in, its young owner was trying hard to establish historical credentials. "The inside is new, to be sure," he informed me (I noted a jukebox and a *bar Américain*), "but the walls remain from the original Café du Commerce. I could show you the deed. Unfortunately, the notary who has it is absent. Do you see that flat rock just outside? Napoleon sat on it. Absolutely. It was a Monday—market day—and a peasant woman brought him two eggs . . ."

Corps. "I come from a long line of wigmakers and barbers," said Emma Martin, the aged waitress who served me lunch at the Hôtel de la Poste. "When Napoleon was staying in the Auberge Dumas—it became the *gendarmerie*—my great-grandmother Josephine shaved him." Her honest, plaintive face put skepticism to shame. "If monsieur cares to wait until I clear the tables, I have something at home that may interest him."

I chatted, meanwhile, with the hotel manager. Any of the old Corps families, he assured me, could confirm

Among these Napoleonic sweets, created by an enterprising chef in Gap, is a "Grognard," or "grumbler," as Napoleon's campaigners were popularly called.

A satirical print shows Napoleon approaching Paris in an eagle-drawn chariot, as city officials sourly look on.

"Here on Monday, March 6, 1815, returning from Elba, the Emperor Napoleon paused," says a Saint-Bonnet monument.

Emma's tale. Her duties done, she led me along a cobblestone street to her lodgings, one small dark room, and from a glass cupboard took down a kidney-shaped china mug and a copper pot. "The very ones my great-grandmother Josephine used to shave Napoleon," she said reverently. "The pot was for mixing the soap and water, and she held the mug under his chin to catch the dripping."

Laffrey. "The Field of the Encounter." The crisis. On a hillock between the road to Grenoble and the Lake of Laffrey the equestrian statue faces the field, the rider serene, the horse lifting a fore and hind hoof in the attitude of a brisk trot. Few Frenchmen approach the site without a surge of pride.

Grenoble, fifteen miles ahead and guarding the gateway to the north, was one of the country's most heavily fortified cities. Behind its ramparts General Marchand waited with two full regiments of the line and companies from three others, a total of six thousand troops. Knowing that many of them had fought under Napoleon and still idolized him, Marchand feared defections if he marched out to meet him in full force. Instead he dispatched a company of sappers and a battalion of the 5th Line Regiment, about eight hundred men, under an officer of unblemished Royalist record, Major Delessart, to cut the bridge spanning the Bonne River before Napoleon reached it. But the mayor of that locality, a Bonapartist, dissuaded Delessart by pleading that destruction would make no difference; the enemy, so he argued, could easily ford the river. The detachment withdrew to Laffrey. Captain Randon, the nineteen-year-old Royalist who commanded the front rank of riflemen, told Delessart, "No doubt of it, we'll have to shoot him down."

Toward eleven o'clock on the morning of March 7 Napoleon crossed the river in an open coach behind a column of Polish lancers, with Tauris, led by the bridle, walking alongside.

An hour later Laffrey came into view. As thousands of civilians looked on from the heights, the Royalist troops closed ranks, their rifles at the ready. Napoleon, who from the beginning had played for the long-range political advantages of a bloodless victory, sent two officers forward under a flag of truce. Delessart repulsed them. Mustering his peerless talents as a gambler and an actor, Napoleon ordered his lancers to fall back and his grenadiers to carry their guns harmlessly under their left arms. Then he mounted his charger and advanced alone. "There he is!" shouted Randon. "Fire!" The riflemen took aim. "Soldiers of the Fifth," Napoleon called out, reining his horse within point-blank range. "I am your Emperor. Don't you recognize me?" He threw open his greatcoat, exposing his bemedaled chest. "If any one among you wants to kill his Emperor, here I am."

There was an instant of deathly stillness. Then as from a single throat burst the cry: *"Vive l'Empereur!"* Ripping off their white cockades, twirling their shakos on the points of their bayonets, the soldiers broke ranks and swarmed around him. Randon took to his horse and galloped away. Delessart, in tears, surrendered his sword to Napoleon. The gambler had won again. With his army stronger by eight hundred defectors, he swept on to Grenoble. After a token resistance General Marchand decamped, and the exultant garrison opened the gates.

I was struck by the irony of the warning fastened to the fence surrounding the equestrian statue: "Insecurely balanced. No approach allowed."

Grenoble. The Hôtel Napoleon at 7 rue Montorge—in Napoleon's day, the Trois Dauphins—is alone among the dozens so renamed with an unassailable certificate of authenticity. The municipal archives firmly establish room No. 3, first floor front, as the one the Emperor occupied for three days. I had telephoned ahead to the manager to reserve the room for me.

It is an unassuming hotel. Room No. 3 contains the minimum of shabby furniture. No rug covers the floor boards. A curtain hides a washbasin and bidet. When I asked about a bathroom, the manager reminded me, "You insisted on this room. Napoleon had no bath either."

But from No. 3 there does project a balcony, classic accessory of demagogic oratory, and stepping out, I imagined how perfectly its situation suited Napoleon. Facing a big public park, it hangs so low that I could almost have touched the passers-by. Napoleon spent a good deal of time on it, whipping the populace into a frenzy of adoration. "At Golfe-Juan," he wrote in his memoirs, "I was but an adventurer; at Grenoble I was a prince."

Bourgoin. Neither nature nor man interposed any further obstacles. After Grenoble the terrain was flat, the road straight, and the populace fanatically pro-Bonaparte. On some days the army covered as much as fifty miles. The Hôtel du Parc, now the Hôtel César, provided another bedroom with balcony, from which Napoleon rallied more recruits. The present owner-chef, Jean Chevenas, whose parents inhabit the room, told me the traditional story of one ardent matriarch's sacrifice: she offered Napoleon all seven of her sons. "That's more than a mother can spare," he said. "I'll send two of them back to you."

Lyon. He acted as though he were already re-enthroned. Formally resuming the title of emperor, he commandeered a suite in the archbishop's palace (today the municipal library), from which King Louis's brother, the Comte d'Artois, had fled that morning. Constantly taking snuff from a box with a miniature of his Austrian empress, Marie-Louise, on the lid, Napoleon received the homage of the clergy, the city councilors, the academicians. He issued decrees. He reviewed troops, playfully pulling the old campaigners' ears and cuffing them. Bonapartist mobs smashed the windows of Royalist houses. "*Lyonnais,*" cried the Emperor, "I love you!"

Villefranche-sur-Saône. Every village within a radius of twenty-five miles was deserted; the inhabitants had flocked here to acclaim Napoleon. After he lunched on chicken at the Town Hall (still used as such), a relic-mad provincial bribed the caterer to give him the bones.

Mâcon. Of the Hôtel du Sauvage (long vanished), where Napoleon stayed overnight, a contemporary travelers' guide notes: "The innkeeper's wife is pretty, amiable, friendly, and contributes singularly to the glory of her husband."

Tournus. My sense of time and space was undergoing a pleasant dislocation. The old families I visited spoke of Napoleon's passage with such intimacy, such immediacy, that it might have happened yesterday. Nowhere does the past more vividly haunt the present than at the Clos Putigny, the manor to which Baron Jean-Marie Putigny took his bride after his years of combat in Napoleon's campaigns, including Waterloo. Created a baron by the Emperor himself at Regensburg, and decorated with the cross of the Légion d'Honneur, he typified the gristly, stand-fast Anglophobe *grognard* ("grumbler, as Napoleon's veterans of the Old Guard were known). Shortly before his death in 1849, at the age of seventy-five, Baron Putigny wrote his memoirs, concluding them thus: "Before long, leaning on my wife's arm, I shall no longer be able to walk around my garden. Nor tomorrow perhaps, to leave my armchair. And so will end the last march. Then the great cry of victory and of the dying will rise to my old lips: VIVE L'EMPEREUR!"

The indomitable soldier's great-granddaughter, Madame Louis Miot, now lived at the Clos Putigny with her octogenarian husband, who, like his forebears for five centuries, had been a prominent notary of the region. Taking me to the baron's bedroom, kept as he left it, she said, "The house was built during the reign of Louis XVI, and the moment he settled here he removed the royal fleur-de-lis motif from the chimney place and redecorated the whole room in Empire style. This is his portrait as a young officer." The head is long and thin, the brow lofty, the eyes defiant. He wears the cross of the Légion d'Honneur over his heart. "And this is the bed he died in." On the wall over the headboard hung a heavy Hanoverian sword that he had retrieved from a Dutch battlefield and fought with ever after, killing 154 men, two of them in duels. When he sheathed it for the last time, he tied a label to the haft: "With this sword I had the consolation, the day after the catastrophe at Waterloo, of killing one of the last enemies."

The Miots' son, Hubert Miot-Putigny, as he proudly signs himself, a journalist whom I later met in Paris, continued the family reminiscences. "When Napoleon's remains were returned from Saint Helena for entombment in the Invalides, Baron Putigny put on his old uniform and followed by coach. He was sixty-six then, it was winter, and he contracted pneumonia and rheumatism, which left him partly paralyzed. He owned a cockatoo named Coco, whom he taught to curse the Bourbons and praise Bonaparte, and on market days he would sit by the gates of the estate, encouraging the bird to screech its vilest obscenities. I knew Coco myself in my early boyhood. Yes, he lived, incredibly, until 1913, sixty-four years longer than his master. His feathers were almost gone and his voice reduced to a whisper, but I can still hear him feebly croaking, '*Plan-plan-rataplan! Vive l'Empereur!*'"

Chalon-sur-Saône. The heart of the

Burgundy wine country. In a glass of *Clos Vougeot* I toasted the memory of Napoleon's Colonel Bisson, who, during an earlier march, passed that noble vineyard and commanded his regiment to halt and salute.

Autun. An empty gray tourist bus stood like a broken-winded elephant before the Hôtel Saint-Louis et Poste. I arrived too late to book Napoleon's room. Two American ladies had retained it weeks ahead, but they cheerfully let me have a look. Nobody knows which of the two Empire beds was Napoleon's. Neither measures much more than five feet, so that the Little Corporal risked bumping his head. The American ladies told me they had to sleep with their knees drawn up. They were nevertheless enchanted. The bedside tables and oil lamps all date from the First Empire; to avoid any taint of modernity, the telephone was placed in the bathroom.

Napoleon was distinctly annoyed by his reception here. The inhabitants failed to cheer him and kept their windows shut. The mayor had gone so far as to issue a proclamation against him. Summoning all the town dignitaries to the hotel, the Emperor gave them a fearful tongue lashing. "But, after all, Sire," said the president of the Civil Tribunal, "you *did* abdicate." "Quiet!" shouted Napoleon. "You're nothing but a rotten attorney."

Avallon. In the hands of the present owner the Hôtel de la Poste has garnered a 🏰 ("top class") and its restaurant ✿✿ ("excellent cuisine, worth a detour") in the *Guide Michelin*. A keg-shaped man with the pursy mouth of the professional gourmet, René Hure bought the resplendent seventeenth-century mansion in 1944 after the Germans finished using it as regional headquarters. It abounds in Napoleonic mementos. Hure's personal collection includes uniforms and arms. But the *pièce de résistance* is the balconied suite, combining rooms 2 and

"Fire!" ordered the Royalist captain at Laffrey. But Napoleon cried out to the soldiers, "I am your Emperor!" Whereupon they flocked to his side, and the captain fled. Later that year, the triumphant scene was immortalized in this painting by Charles Steuben.

81

The joyful Grenoblois *removed the city gates and brought them to the hero, who greeted his admirers from this balcony.*

The balcony and the room are in what is now the Hotel Napoléon. Grenoble is still proud of having welcomed Napoleon.

On March 20 Napoleon at last entered Paris, escorted, according to this print, by a trumpeting Victory and an eagle.

3, that Napoleon chose. "It wasn't his first visit," Hure told me. "He stayed here on three previous occasions, once in 1802, with Josephine."

Wonderful news greeted the Emperor at the hotel. The mighty Marshal Ney, who had left Paris promising King Louis to "bring Napoleon back in an iron cage," had announced his submission to the Emperor and was marching to join him with six thousand troops.

Auxerre. "Kiss me, Ney," said Napoleon, as he welcomed the defecting marshal at the prefecture. They marched on together, their combined forces totaling twenty thousand. (In Paris a message purporting to be from Napoleon to Louis XVIII was pasted to the Vendôme Column: "My good brother, no use sending me more troops, I have enough.")

Joigny. The elderly librarian was still indignant. "Do you know what he said," she asked me, her wattles quivering, "when the whole town turned out to acclaim him, everybody except the nobility? He said, 'Is there nothing but scum in this place?'"

Pont-sur-Yonne. At Auxerre on the river Yonne, Napoleon had embarked a number of his troops on barges. Since navigation by dark was hazardous in those waters, the vessels anchored at Pont-sur-Yonne for the night. "Are you afraid of getting wet?" he chided the pilots. The soldiers thereupon insisted on chancing it. One barge shattered against a bridge post, drowning all hands. It is said that as the grenadiers sank, they could be heard shouting with their last breath, *"Vive l'Empereur!"*

Meanwhile Napoleon imposed himself on the Royalist Comte de Broussillon, stretching out fully dressed for a nap in a bedroom of his house. The countess refused to speak to the intruder. It amused him nevertheless to force on her the gift of one of his monogrammed handkerchiefs.

At Avallon, as though guided by the Michelin, *Napoleon of course stopped at the Hôtel de la Poste. He was given this suite, now adorned with his portrait bust.*

German bombs flattened the house in 1940. Mayor Brisson, who managed to rescue an Empire mirror from the wreckage and hang it in the Town Hall, showed me the remnants of the foundation.

Fontainebleau. Crossing the Place du Château—recently renamed the Place du Général de Gaulle—Napoleon entered his old quarters in the palace as casually as if he had never left them. (They consisted of an antechamber for his guards, his secretary's office, his study, bedroom, and a bath with a zinc tub encased in mahogany.) When he arrived, he learned that Louis was gone. The press of the day provides a stunning example of journalistic accommodation. Two days earlier the *Journal des Débats* had compared Napoleon to Genghis Khan and Attila the Hun, "only more odious." Two days later, adopting the name *Journal de l'Empire*, it reported, "Paris has the aspect of security and joy." After Waterloo it resumed its former title.

Paris. At nine o'clock on the evening of March 20 Napoleon's coach rolled through the Tuileries gates. The crowd was so demonstrative that he cried, "You're suffocating me, my friends!"

The Emperor and his army completed the journey from beach to palace in twenty days, less than half the time that it ordinarily required then. As travel-frayed myself as my Peugeot looked, I couldn't carp at his own appraisal of the expedition—"the most prodigious march of which history has any record."

John Kobler is the author of Luce: His Time, Life and Fortune (*Doubleday and Company*); *he is working on a biography of Teilhard de Chardin.*

The Wonder of the World

Frederick II of Hohenstaufen was perhaps the most gifted ruler in all the centuries between Charlemagne and Napoleon. As an emperor he failed, but as a one-man Renaissance he brought light and learning to a dark world

Italy south of Naples is the Mezzogiorno—the land of the noonday sun. In the Mezzogiorno ignorance and poverty seem endemic. Not many travelers even in our day penetrate there. The land is craggy, barren, and disease-ridden; and the north—the Italy of avant-garde films, *la dolce vita,* and aggressive modern capitalism—seems far away. In the south the traditions of organized banditry and vendetta still endure; the peasants are sunk in a kind of sullen apathy that even the communists cannot shake.

There has been little of love and compassion in the history of the Mezzogiorno. But it was not always a wasteland. Nine hundred years ago in this forgotten region of Europe the Moslem East, Byzantium, and the barbarian North all fused together in a civilization of wealth, glitter, and intellectual brilliance under the Norman kings of Sicily. And here in the thirteenth century a grand ideological drama was played out: the dream of a united, powerful, and ultimately secular Europe (a dream of our own time)

This portrait of Frederick II, stupor mundi, *is the frontispiece from his book on falconry. The lily he holds in his hand may be a symbol of imperial power.*

clashed with an older dream of God's universal order on earth. In the events of this drama we can discern the collision of the skeptical spirit of the yet-distant Renaissance with the static, believing spirit of the Middle Ages.

Yet it is not quite so. The roles and characters of the actors are oddly mixed, so that the worldliness of popes is matched by the brutal despotism of the champions of a secular empire. In the end neither side won. The dream of secular society went down in a welter of futility and blood. The religious vision was painfully corrupted by the desperate struggle for survival, dooming itself in the aftermath of ostensible victory to the contempt of believing and thinking men.

It is a drama rich in personalities—great medieval popes and kings. But the single greatest figure of the drama, indeed perhaps the single greatest figure of the thirteenth century, was Frederick II of Hohenstaufen, Holy Roman Emperor, king of Sicily, king of Jerusalem, lecher, scientist, political prophet, mathematician, lawmaker, poet, linguist, sinner thrice excommunicated and consigned by Dante to hell to roast forever in an incandescent tomb; a man known to his contemporaries, without the slightest flat-

tery, as *stupor mundi,* "the wonder of the world."

If, seven hundred years later, there is any touching feature to this terrible drama, it is an aging woman's love for the defenseless child born late in her life, and the love of the man that child became for the Mezzogiorno. For Frederick, Italy, especially the south, was the soul of the world and ultimately the cause of his ruination. To him Apulia, Lucania, Calabria, and Sicily were *il Regno, the* kingdom, "a haven," as he put it, "amidst the floods and a pleasure garden amidst a waste of thorns." At the height of his career, straddling Europe and the Levant, he marveled that God had flattered Palestine so when he might have loved Italy instead.

Every biography must begin with the banal fact of birth. Frederick Roger of Hohenstaufen was born in the Italian hill town of Iesi on the day after Christmas, A.D. 1194. But there was nothing banal in the circumstances of his birth nor in his inheritance. On his paternal side he was a Hohenstaufen—a family that the popes at Rome, with a unanimity born of experience, called the devil's brood. His grandfather was Frederick I, called Barbarossa, generally conceded

By EDMUND STILLMAN

85

Castel del Monte in Apulia

The Cuba palace in Palermo's royal park

by historians to have been the greatest of the German Holy Roman Emperors, a man who had fought to stalemate the pretensions of the papacy and who so seized the imagination of his time that later generations insisted that Barbarossa had not died on crusade but instead slept with his warriors in the bowels of the Kyffhäuser mountain, whence he would emerge on his great war horse when the German people called.

Frederick's father was Henry VI, a man devoid of Barbarossa's largeness of style but one just as ambitious, a cold-blooded intriguer and killer hated by wife and family, whose short reign was spent in an incessant struggle for the hegemony of Europe and whose early death less than three years after Frederick's birth was greeted by the papacy with profoundest relief.

More attractive perhaps, but no softer, was his mother's legacy. On his mother's side Frederick was Norman, but not of the house of the Norman kings of England. Constance was a princess of a different line, the last legitimate representative of a clan of Norman freebooters who had descended on Italy like wolves in the eleventh century, serving as faithless mercenaries to Byzantine and Lombard overlords, fattening on the incessant warfare they helped to foment in the southern marches of Christendom. Finally, in the glittering figures of Robert Guiscard and his brother Roger they had seized Sicily and southern Italy, a domain that dwarfed the roughly contemporary conquest of England in the cold North Atlantic: the commerce of the port of Palermo yielded more revenue to Count Roger of Sicily than the Normans could extract from all of twelfth-century England. And Palermo was only a part of the much greater whole—a kingdom built on the threefold heritage of the Byzantine emperors at Constantinople who had held the island and southern Italy for centuries, the Saracen emirs of Sicily, and the restless North.

Frederick's mother was at the time of her marriage to Henry Hohenstaufen a spinster of thirty-one, long since reconciled to a life of barren piety; some said she had become a nun. But when it appeared she would fall heir, in her plain person, to the gorgeous Norman patrimony, she was judged a fit wife even for a future Holy Roman Emperor, eleven years her junior, who aspired to govern the world. Miraculously, after nine childless years of marriage Constance gave birth to Frederick at Iesi—in a pavilion erected in the market place in plain sight of hundreds of townsmen, so we are told, lest there be any question thereafter of the legitimate birth of her son. Other chroniclers record only that fifteen cardinals and bishops stood crowded in the tent and were judged sufficient witness to the point.

Like many a latecomer to motherhood, Constance proved a doting parent. Frederick, so the chroniclers record, was everything to her, and though Dante has placed her in paradise as the very type of the devout and dutiful woman, there is an ugly suspicion that she did not stick at intriguing for the murder of her hated husband in order to advance her son to the throne. The plot, real or imagined, was betrayed to Henry, and young Frederick may have been exposed to the sight of the tortures inflicted on the suspects. There was to be no shortage of torture in Frederick's life.

The Norman kings of Sicily had been vassals of the popes. They had gained a dubious legitimacy by swearing to be the popes' men, and whatever the extent of their ambitions and

"OUR PLACES OF SOLACE"

In architecture as in all else, Frederick sought to blend the Oriental with the European. As a boy he lived at times in the Cuba, shown opposite as it must have looked about 1200, when it was one of the chief Arabo-Norman pleasure domes of Palermo. As a man Frederick built his own pleasure domes in southern Italy—"*loca solatiorum nostrum*," he called them: "our places of solace." The most famous was Castel del Monte, opposite at left, an octagon of limestone with eight octagonal towers. Frederick may have borrowed this plan from the Moslem architects of Palestine. Another of the imperial solaces, called Gioia del Colle, was built near Bari. Its throne, at right, is decorated with carvings after the Persian style.

E.N.I.T.

The throne room at the castle of Gioia del Colle

their later perfidies, they had mainly directed their avarice and longing, not against the secular domain of the popes in central Italy, but against the Moslems and Byzantines of the East. As the popes' men—and formidable warriors they were—they had fought the German emperors, who wanted to recreate the long-dead Roman Empire in the implausible guise of a union of Germany and Italy. For the popes, who aspired to a countersupremacy over the worldly power of kings and yet exercised only an insecure territorial sovereignty of their own in central Italy—the *patrimonium Petri*—it was a condition of survival to keep the Holy Roman emperors at bay. Now the popes' Norman shield was gone, for by marrying Constance and gaining her Sicilian inheritance, a German emperor had achieved at last what it had always been papal policy to prevent. He had turned the popes' southern flank; his rival, the spiritual power of Rome, was thus caught between hammer and anvil.

The papacy was saved by Henry's sudden death, from dysentery, in 1197. This was for the papacy an almost miraculous deliverance. But for the three-year-old Frederick his father's death was a personal catastrophe: his mother, worn out by years and anxiety, was herself in poor health and, sensing her approaching death, could think of nothing better to do than, in desperation, commit the child to the care of Pope Innocent III. In her last act of policy Frederick was crowned king at Palermo in May, 1198, and six months later his mother was dead.

The guardianship of the pope was casual. A rival unfriendly to Frederick succeeded to the throne of the Holy Roman Empire. The kingdom of Sicily, which was Frederick's sole inheritance, fell into anarchy, and the boy himself was left to run wild in the streets of Palermo. Frederick may not actually have gone hungry—the poor townsfolk are said to have fed him from their meager stores—but he learned about neglect and want. Yet some of his most attractive qualities surely stem from his years as a barefooted *ragazzo* of Palermo. These were his quickness of wit, his self-reliance, and the determination to prevail; he acquired as well a polyglot command of French, Arabic, Greek, and Italian and a permanent addiction to the lands of the sun.

Frederick might have died of neglect or as the victim of obscure political murder if the new Holy Roman Emperor, Otto of the Welf house of Brunswick, had proved faithful to his pledges. A member of a family who were sworn enemies to the Hohenstaufens, Otto had taken power as a friend to the popes, promising to submit to the spiritual authority of the church. But once again the office made the man: a pliant tool before his coronation as emperor, after he held power Otto undertook the conquest of Sicily. Pope Innocent III, faced with the need to undercut his imperial rival, remembered the dirty, half-starving *ragazzo* of Palermo, by now almost grown. He excommunicated Otto and had Frederick elected emperor. Three years later, in 1214, Otto was defeated by the French king, who was acting on the pope's behalf. Frederick's fortunes were made.

Innocent III has been hailed as one of the three greatest of the medieval popes. He was the man who presided over the rise of the Franciscan and Dominican orders; he hammered at the Waldensian heretics and engineered the great crusade against the Albigensian heretics of southern France; he saw the Greek schismatics of Byzantium humbled by the fourth crusade. Fortunately for his peace of mind he

FREDERICK'S BOOK OF FALCONRY

Thirteenth-century monarchs were not expected to be accomplished writers, much less scientists, so it is all the more extraordinary that Frederick himself wrote the book that is regarded as the first work of modern zoology: *De Arte Venandi cum Avibus* (*Of the Art of Hunting with Birds*). It was the standard work on the art of falconry until the eighteenth century, and falconers still consult it.

The book is based on a lifetime study of all kinds of birds, from sparrows to hawks. Their anatomy and plumage, their feeding, mating, and nesting habits, their times and routes of migration—all are so intently observed and well recorded that ornithologists can read the book today with perfect respect.

About nine hundred illustrations were done for the book, probably under Frederick's direction, some possibly by the emperor himself. Of the twelve existing manuscripts, the finest is the one in the Vatican Library, from which the illustrations on these pages are reproduced.

Jesses—leather straps—must be fitted and tied to the falcon's feet, as is shown below. The falconer can then hold the bird on his fist or tie it to a perch or to the edge of a birdbath, as at far right.

Frederick supplies exact recipes for falcon food. You can break an egg into a bowl, as the outdoorsmen are doing above, add a shellful of milk, and cook over a slow fire. Or you can take fresh meat, chop it fine, as at left, and offer it to the falcon on a chopping board (below). Falcons prefer wild birds, but they will also accept domestic fowl.

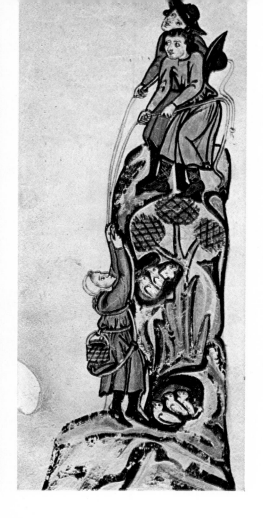

co ligatur ad quiescendū est
de manu deponitur. Sed iuū
autem una e̅ que ptica dicat·

matura quam euomit super
cam: et pream: et miuolutio
que contingit qn̄q̄ iactis fa

Two falconers, at left, lower a companion over the side of a cliff to steal young falcons from an aerie. The technique of tying a falcon to a high perch with a leash is shown above. The swimming falconer below, having piled his clothes on the bank, goes to the rescue of his bird, which has downed its prey on the far side of a pool.

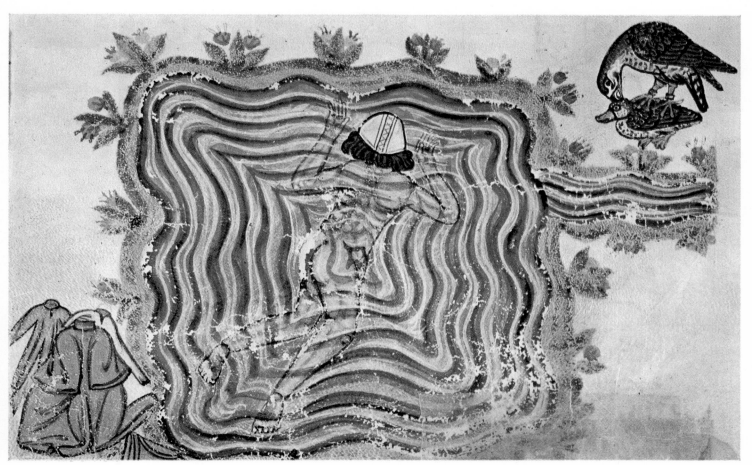

Bathing and dining at Pozzuoli

FREDERICK'S RENAISSANCE MIND

Nothing was beyond the range of Frederick's intellect, but medical practice especially concerned him. He believed in mineral baths and once took a cure at Pozzuoli, a spa near Naples. The bathers and diners at left are from an illustrated poem, dedicated to Frederick, in praise of Pozzuoli. Far in advance of its time was Frederick's code for physicians, which required them to have a diploma and to charge reasonable fees, and forbade them to own a drugstore or to charge the poor *any* fee. In 1231 Frederick chartered the medical school at Salerno. The miniatures opposite are part of a surgical treatise written there. A Renaissance man two centuries before the Renaissance, Frederick admired the ancient Romans. The bust opposite shows him as "Divine Frederick Caesar."

did not live to see his former ward become the deadliest enemy the medieval papacy ever faced; for he died just two years after Otto's defeat. No more than any other ambitious medieval king would Frederick, holding the reality of power, remain a faithful vassal of the popes.

The conflict between the spiritual and the temporal is the leitmotif of medieval history, but it is a curiously ambiguous controversy. The ostensible spiritual contender, the papacy, seeks a temporal authority; and the papacy's temporal enemies, the medieval kings, aspire to a spiritual dominion as well.

To us, seven hundred years later, the terms of the struggle are strange, though they may be made a little more comprehensible by the observation that behind this battle between two abstract conceptions of government lay a conflict involving cold cash as well. The medieval church was vast in its holdings, and each increment to its revenues and prerogatives was a diminution of those of the secular lords. Yet the prize was more than real estate or hard cash. In the medieval mind there was an almost magical conception of man's place in nature and of the honor that fell to

the one who disposed over the rule of mankind.

By the late Middle Ages the papacy had acquired such administrative expertise and power that the popes claimed supreme authority. What was the pope? "The royal High Priest of the Christian church, the *verus imperator* of the Christian Empire, the first judge of Christendom, these three are one and of one origin: they are the Pope," writes the modern German historian Ernst Kantorowicz. "The pope . . . was not . . . the representative of any man, but the representative of Christ himself, and through him the representative of God." According to one medieval propagandist, Manegold of Lautenbach, the Holy Roman Emperor was, by contrast, no more than a swineherd.

Yet the kings of this world, not surprisingly, were unwilling to see themselves as mere swineherds, agents of papal authority and direction. Indeed, for Frederick especially, the emperor was himself the earthly incarnation of divine justice and power. Condemning to unspeakable torture those who had plotted his death, Frederick, then at the height of his career, proclaimed that the criminals had not merely struck at his own person: by striking

at the emperor the traitors had "imperilled the fabric of the world." In this view, as Kantorowicz puts it, "If God is present on earth . . . [and] has condescended to reveal himself as Justice in unconsecrated precincts, the State can no longer be conceived as 'sinful,' a relative good amid the total evil of the world; but becomes forthwith an absolute good in its own right." It is for this reason that such progenitors of modern German autocracy as Nietzsche and the historian Treitschke hailed Frederick for his politics and that in our time the Nazis cited him as an early incarnation of the *Führerprinzip*.

This much at least of the bitter controversy is easily comprehensible to us today. And to the degree that emperor and pope quarreled not about the mere division of earthly revenues but about the nature of conscience, the role of the state, and indeed about the nature of man as a social animal—inherently reasonable or inherently bestial and standing in need of constant brutal correction—their quarrel is relevant even to our own time.

But for Frederick it was no mere abstract controversy. Any biographer of Frederick must reckon with the

Medicine at Frederick's university: three steps in the treatment of a head wound

Frederick in the guise of a Caesar

fact that this stupendous talent and imagination were marred by megalomania. At his best, Frederick was an intellect two or three centuries in advance of his time—as skeptical a scientific theorist as Francis Bacon, as daring a political schemer as Cesare Borgia. If he was not a compassionate man, he was nevertheless capable of tolerance for men of all faiths. But at his worst, Frederick was a man who could chop off the thumb of a scribe for misspelling the imperial name and condemn his oldest friend, suspected of treason, to hideous torture. Frederick was less concerned with the abstract issue of spiritual power versus secular than with *his* majesty, *his* prerogatives, *his* near divinity. Frederick foreshadowed not only the intellectual achievements but the manic pride of the High Renaissance. In the pious medieval environment he came perilously close to blasphemy when he saw in himself a kind of second Christ, incarnate in the person of the Holy Roman Emperor, ruler of the world; so that the little town of Iesi where Frederick was born became, in his words, "our Bethlehem," and he proclaimed that portents had attended his birth.

The court that Frederick maintained in the south was one of the most brilliant in history. Nothing like it had been seen in the Christian West before, not even in the great days of Charlemagne. The rude court of that Frankish emperor could not boast steam baths and plumbing to rival those of ancient Rome, a menagerie of wild beasts from distant Africa and India, a wholly secular university that challenged the intellectual monopoly of the medieval church, and a secular bureaucracy that was the product of this education and that regulated the foreign commerce into the port of Palermo down to the finest detail. It was a court where for the first time poets, as Dante noted approvingly a century later, sang a sophisticated early verse in the Italian vernacular. There eunuchs guarded harems of Moorish women, and the pious were daily offended by the brazen comings and goings of infidel Moslem and Jewish alchemists, philosophers, astrologers, and mathematicians.

In intellectual terms the court of Frederick deserves nothing but praise. In an age hopelessly wed to the supernatural, the brilliant Frederican courts at Palermo, Foggia, and Castel del Monte truly justified the epithet the age applied to Frederick—*stupor mundi et immutator mirabilis,* "wonder of the world and marvelous innovator."

Some of the greatest names of medieval humanism and science revolved in Frederick's orbit. Among them were the jurist and polemicist Pietro della Vigna, the mathematician Leonardo Fibonacci, who is said to have introduced to Europe Arabic numerals and the concept of the zero, and the astrologer and philosopher Michael Scot. These men, together with a learned slave reportedly sent to Frederick by the sultan of Egypt, examined the mysteries of the natural world. Why, asked Frederick, puzzling over the phenomenon of the refraction of light, does a lance in water appear bent? Why does the sun appear red as it nears the horizon?

Frederick's curiosity was limitless and wholly unconstrained by such few notions of mercy as lighted a savage age. One monkish chronicler relates that Frederick, "Wanting to find out what kind of speech children would have when they grew up, if they spoke to no one before hand . . . bade foster mothers and nurses to suckle the children, to bathe and wash them, but in no way to prattle with

White-hot tombs in the sixth ring of the Inferno

them, for he wanted to learn whether they would speak the Hebrew language, which was the oldest, or Greek, or Latin, or Arabic, or perhaps the language of their parents, of whom they had been born. But he labored in vain, because the children all died. For they could not live without the petting and the joyful faces and loving words of their foster mothers."

His excursions into ornithology were less self-defeating. He was enough a man of his time to share a passion for the hunt, or at least for the art of falconry, but he was apart from his time in his intelligent and detached curiosity about birds and all their ways. For his illegitimate son Manfred he compiled a great compendium of knowledge on birds, not merely falcons: his work deals with skeletal structure, plumage, and the presumed mechanics of flight, as well as with the training of falcons and their diseases. "Our intention is to set forth the things which are, as they are," he writes, establishing the empiricist's credo. "We have often experimented." Aristotle and the authority of the ancients did not overawe him. "We have followed Aristotle where necessary," he writes, "but we have learned from experience that he appears frequently to deviate from the truth. . . ."

But for all his protomodernity Frederick emerges more as the type of an Oriental potentate than as the common variety of medieval king or Renaissance despot. Indeed, it was in the Levant, where, bowing to intense papal pressure, he undertook a serio-comic crusade to liberate the Holy Land, that Frederick seems to have found his spiritual home. The histrionics of medieval crusading clearly bored him, and it is an ironic comment on the brave but bumbling military operations of the times that this cynical atheist, who contemptuously dismissed the holiness of the Sepulcher, should have accomplished more by skillful negotiation (in Arabic, to the entranced delight of his enemies) than all his earnest but inept contemporaries could accomplish by their battles. What did Frederick care for the cause itself? The answer must be nothing. "There have been three great impostors in history," he once wearily observed. "Moses, Jesus, and Mohammed." Or so his papal enemies swear he blasphemed. Others, knowing Frederick's respect for the Moslems, were less certain he took the Lord Mohammed's name in vain.

If military operations in the Holy Land were to Frederick an ineffable bore, military operations closer to home were not. From the day he secured himself in the *Regno*, returning from a Germany that he chose thenceforth virtually to ignore, he was engaged in incessant war. But this was a war for the glory of the Hohenstaufens, waged against the insolent communes of central and northern Italy allied to Frederick's enemies. Delivery of the Holy Sepulcher was no part of Frederick's true interest; indeed, so long did he delay in the discharge of this obligation that he was excommunicated for the sin—and then denounced for undertaking the obligation without first making his act of contrition. But the fight to deliver royal power from the challenge of papal pretension and the encroachments of upstart city bourgeoisie and proletarians became his burning political cause.

Frederick in effect was driven to fight in this Italian arena because his larger German ambitions had all been rebuked. The Holy Roman Empire was too huge a conception for political health. The emperors could not, like the French, English, and Spanish kings, secure a territorial base from

FREDERICK ENTOMBED

Dante took care to provide Frederick with a most agonizing place in the sixth ring of Hell. He and other grand-scale heretics were to roast there forever in chests that burned hotter than "iron in the forge of any artificers." The illustration opposite, by Botticelli, shows Dante and Virgil (in multiples) as they hurry past the incandescent tombs from which "came forth such fearful crying, 'twas plain that here sad tortured spirits mourned." Frederick himself chose to be buried as a Christian in this cool tomb of porphyry, near the remains of his parents and his first wife, Constance of Aragon, in the Palermo Cathedral.

Frederick's sarcophagus in Palermo

which in time they could control their unruly barons. Frederick's clan has been criticized for its Italian ambitions; but it was the unsatisfied longing for a compact imperial base, to be used as a springboard for power, that led the Hohenstaufen emperors again and again over the Alps and into Italy. Their hope was always that with a secure Italian base behind them they could strike north once again to assert their rule.

But for them power over Italy was always a will-o'-the-wisp. Their Italian ambitions led them into inevitable collision not only with the popes but also with the cities of Tuscany and the north Lombard plain. Behind their walls, in the thirteenth century, a new world was struggling toward birth. It was a postfeudal world, a society of pushing urban middle classes and proletarians, of new mercantile interests and incipient nationalism—all incompatible with the despotic ambitions of Frederick and his imperial kind.

In the field the citizen armies of the Italian communes were seldom more than a helpless rabble. If caught in the open they inevitably fell victim to the professional arms of Frederick's German and Saracen knights. But such was the primitive state of military art in the thirteenth century that the citizens, behind their walls, were nearly always safe from Frederick's wrath. Time and again he moved against them, and time and again, despite ephemeral successes, the combination of papal denunciation, which undermined his own forces' loyalty, and Lombard doggedness in defense ensured Frederick's failure.

And fail he did. *Stupor mundi*, wonder of the world, outstanding political intelligence of his time though he might be, in collision with these nascent forces he proved helpless. He could not in the end transcend the materials and the inherent limitations of his age.

All the cruelty, all the implacable discharge of hate, the butchery of captured rabble, could not break the spirit of the towns, bolstered as they were by the blessing of the popes and by their own will to resist. Frederick might love his Italy, but to the Italians he was a German king. He died in 1250, a defeated and bitterly disappointed man. He had built the first secular European state, codified laws, regulated commerce, fostered progress in the governmental interest, challenged medieval obscurantism and ec-

clesiastical pretension; but his work did not live long beyond him.

His two surviving legitimate sons had proved either weak or traitorous. Neither was competent to succeed Frederick. Into the vacuum in Italy moved the best of his sons—that Manfred for whom he had written the falconry book, Frederick's bastard by his beloved Bianca Lancia. Manfred intrigued bloodily for his father's legacy. For twelve years he maintained the semblance of Frederick's glories in southern Italy, only to be defeated and killed in 1266 by a great French punitive expedition that invaded Italy at papal request. The Hohenstaufen line—the devil's brood—was virtually at an end.

What Frederick built did not endure. Viewed in retrospect, his dream of a powerful secular empire could never have succeeded, though Frederick would have done anything in the wild pursuit of his vision. For him no brutality, no breach of faith, was too much. But his vision was out of its time. It is almost as if history had made a bizarre experiment and then had dropped it for another. The future lay with the middle-class, urban, capitalistic society that was then struggling into being in Italy.

Tucked away in the bleak Himalaya, the Buddhist monastery of Lamayaru squats in a valley 13,500 feet above sea level near Ladakh

MR. SINGH GOES TO THE HIMALAYA

The bold, mystical paintings reproduced on the following pages have never before been seen in color outside the Himalayan temple-fortresses in which they were painted. They were photographed by a most venturesome scholar, Madanjeet Singh, a long-time student of Asian art and a member of India's diplomatic corps. To obtain the photographs, Mr. Singh made thirty-five expeditions over the period of a year, by helicopter, jeep, and pony—and by foot through the harrowing mountain paths. The expeditions were nothing if not eventful. Once, in the midst of a blizzard, Mr. Singh found himself racing through a pass to avoid being snowed in for the winter; another time he stood with his hands prayerfully over his head as an avalanche rumbled behind him in the dark; and once he tumbled over the side of a cliff, to be saved only by a sturdy bush ten feet below. He was able to overcome the religious ban on taking photographs in the monasteries by obtaining a letter of introduction from the most revered figure in Himalayan Buddhism, the Dalai Lama, now an exile from Tibet. The letter had miraculous results: the monks knelt, kissed it, and permitted Mr. Singh to set up his equipment in the temples. The result of all these adventures will be *Himalayan Art*, Mr. Singh's fifth book, from which the paintings reproduced here were selected. It is the first of a new series in the "UNESCO Art Book" collection and will be published in this country by the New York Graphic Society.

Conceive of a modern traveler to some remote corner of northernmost Scandinavia coming upon churches adorned with an art that had died out in civilized Europe many centuries before. Conceive further that the religion inspiring that art is itself a fantastic offshoot of medieval Christian beliefs. A situation as dramatic as this hypothetical one prevails in what is perhaps the last great remote area of the world: the wind-swept, mountain-walled valleys of the Himalaya. Here a branch of Indian Buddhism has made its last stand and with it a strange mystical art that is rarely seen by outsiders.

It is not a folk art growing up in utter isolation; for as remote and nearly inaccessible as the Himalayan regions are, the crosscurrents of history have never quite bypassed them. These currents have reached them slowly, however, in time with the pace

THE HIDDEN ART OF THE HIGH HIMALAYA

Mountain demons and Hindu deities
merge with the Buddhist
vision in these magical paintings

By MADANJEET SINGH

The Buddha meditates in a superb Himalayan painting from Bhutan

of the trade caravans that still traverse the deep river valleys and the tortuous passes of Ladakh, Himachal Pradesh, Nepal, Bhutan, and Sikkim. It was the caravans and pilgrims that carried the culture of India into the Himalaya, predominantly from the Buddhist centers of Kashmir and the great monastic institutions of the Ganges basin in Bihar and Bengal. As Buddhism fanned out through the Himalaya to become the religion of all Asia, its art models, carried on painted banners by pilgrims, also traversed the "silk routes" of Central Asia and later reached Tibet, whence they slowly turned back upon the Himalayan kingdoms of Bhutan and Sikkim as late as the fifteenth and sixteenth centuries—a one-millennium journey covering a linear distance of about six hundred miles. It is as if the love songs of medieval Provence had finally reached the Hebrides last year.

Geography sufficiently explains the slow pace of change, for these mountains comprise a natural barrier surrounded by barriers. On their southeastern borders, where the Himalaya give way to the Indian plains, are vast malarial swamps and impenetrable savannas of fifteen-foot-high elephant grass. On the northern borders of the Himalaya at least forty mountain peaks average twenty thousand feet. Between these two borders lie roaring river gorges and rain-pelted valleys hemmed in by sheer mountain walls and rolling, barren ranges. Each valley is a world unto itself, because for the most part one is linked to another by nothing save perilous footpaths, an occasional mule track, and dizzying rope bridges. Such a topography has naturally sheltered and nourished inbred ideas and "timeless" symbols.

The Buddhist faith is the inspiration

and reason for Himalayan art—but the form of Buddhism that was carried to the mountains around the eighth century A.D. by the Indian guru Padmasambhava bears scant resemblance to the simple teachings that had been set forth about twelve hundred years before by the historic Buddha, Siddhartha Gautama. What the Himalayan people received was Buddhism in the vastly elaborated form it had taken during its long settlement in India. By the early years of the Christian Era the historic Buddha was deified and elevated into an eternal, absolute, primordial principle. At the same time Indian Buddhism not only permitted the use of idols but took over a vast array of deities from the Hindu religion. The branch of Buddhism that became most popular in the Himalaya was Vajrayana. Vajrayana worship relied on magical formulas and magical cere-

95

monies—and on the introduction of goddesses (Taras) and Buddhas-to-be (Bodhisattvas) to the ever-expanding Buddhist pantheon. Popularly known as Lamaism, this branch of the religion taught that the devotee could summon up a huge number of imagined deities by means of certain magical formulas.

Presumably a novice monk could better fix his imagination if the source of power was pictured in paintings and sculptures, and therefore the deities were described iconographically in the treatises of the fourth and fifth centuries (the Gupta period), and later in even greater detail in the mystical Indian texts known as Tantras. These demigods in the Vajrayana pantheon essentially revolve around the five Dhyani Buddhas, identified with the four points of the compass and the cosmic apex, presided over by the supreme god, the Adi-Buddha. In this way, through the doctrine of an increasingly complex metaphysical thought, the Buddhist pantheon, which had begun with no god at all, was joined by hundreds of "emanations."

Both in Hindu and in Buddhist Tantric beliefs, the duality of the sexes was developed with particular emphasis. One of the cardinal doctrines was the worship of the spiritual-sexual principle: the union of opposites. Dhyana, or meditation as abstract thought, was regarded as the male principle, which remained inert until activated by a cosmic female energy (Shakti, or Prajna). The worship could be sometimes quite literal: among many Tantric devotees, sexual ecstasy was held to be the road to release from the bondage of self— and it was achieved in a ritual in which the worshiper could identify with a particular deity. The magical instrument used to compel deities to reveal their spiritual attributes to the worshiper was the Vajra, a diamond or thunderbolt; hence the name Vajrayana (Vehicle of the Thunderbolt).

By the eighth century, when Buddhism reached Tibet, Vajrayana was practically the only form of Buddhism that still survived in India, its strongholds located in such famous monastic institutions of Bengal and Bihar as Nalanda and Vikramashila. From these monasteries Gautama's ancient creed, now metamorphosed into Tantric Buddhism, came to the Himalaya, where

TEXT CONTINUED ON PAGE 105

A PORTFOLIO OF HIMALAYAN PAINTING

Several outstanding examples of the art of the Himalaya are reproduced in the following portfolio.

Nagasena, opposite, is one of the sixteen chief disciples of the historic Buddha. Here, in a painting from a Sikkimese monastery, he bears the begging bowl and mendicant's staff of an Indian monk. The influence of China, a post-Indian force in Himalayan art, is apparent in the background swirl of clouds.

On the next page, in a frenzied scene from a monastery in Sikkim in the central portion of the Himalaya, a fierce-looking deity brandishes a sword in one hand, a flaming torch in the other, and locks his fanged consort in a sexual embrace known as the "yab-yum," or mother-father posture. The wildly flying drapery, churning flames, and fright figures evoke the ecstasy of the final union between meditation as abstract thought—the male principle—and the cosmic female energy.

At the top of page 99 the sensuous figure of the goddess Saraswati—one of the many Hindu deities incorporated directly into the Himalayan Buddhist pantheon—sits astride a swan, her traditional identifying symbol. Below, the array of Buddha's worshipers is part of a large wall painting in the same monastery in Ladakh. The full painting depicts one of the Jatakas, or tales concerning the previous incarnations of the Buddha, that helped spread Buddhism in Asia.

On pages 100–101 is a portion of a vigorous, room-sized mural from the monastery-fortress of Wangdu Phodang, two days' march from Thimbu, capital of Bhutan. It represents various way stations in the Wheel of Life, a grand theme of Buddhist art grounded in the doctrine, originally Hindu, of reincarnation. The slavering beasts, the cruel birds, and the naked human shivering with cold represent the more hellish prospects waiting for those guilty of bad conduct, just as the worthy, semidivine figures in the center represent the result in one's next reincarnation of right conduct in the present one.

The painting at the top of page 102 renders the sexual theme of Tantricism in a more serene form: that of the gentle, part-bird figure of Manda-Pala and his beloved consort. Below it is a painting from the Thikse monastery, Ladakh, depicting the bold, spiky form of an eagle, one of the symbolic forms of the Tantric protective deity, Yamantaka, "slayer of death."

On page 103 animal symbolism is similarly employed at this monastery in a composition showing a mad-eyed horse (a regal symbol) and an eagle carrying human eyeballs. A rope, intended for a noose, and a skull-topped club are grisly symbols of the fierce Yamantaka, not directly depicted.

On the last page of the portfolio is a rendering of one of Tantricism's gods, Vairocana, who is one of the Buddha's favorite disciples. He is represented here in four-headed form and portrayed larger than life-size at a Bhutanese monastery. With his right hand he displays the prescribed boon-conferring gesture, while in his left is his symbol, the wheel. Alongside, the figures of the Buddha are shown making various hand gestures that are known as mudras.

Sinon Monastery, Sikkim: Nagasena. Early 18th cent

Alchi Monastery, Ladakh: Saraswati. 11th-12th century

ABOVE: Alchi Monastery, Ladakh: A Jataka Scene. 11th-12th century
LEFT: Sinon Monastery, Sikkim: A Form of Mortal Buddha. Early 18th century

OVERLEAF: Wangdu Phodang Monastery, Bhutan: Scenes from the Wheel of Life. Late 16th or early 17th century

Turja Bhawani Temple, Nepal: Saint Manda-Pala and Consort. 16th century

Thikse Monastery, Ladakh: Eagle. 15th century

RIGHT: Thikse Monastery, Ladakh: Tantric Symbols. 15th century

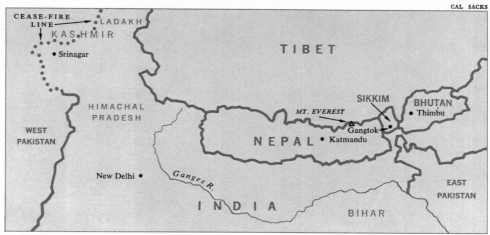

There are few east-west roads through the Himalaya, so that to reach Sikkim from, say, Nepal travelers must—as our author did—first go south to India and then head north.

TEXT CONTINUED FROM PAGE 96

today it still survives, being in fact the state religion of Sikkim and Bhutan.

In the remote monasteries of the Himalaya, Vajrayana, or Tantric Buddhism—and its art—underwent further change, largely in spirit, when it encountered natives who believed then, and believe now, in demons, sorcery, and the pervasive presence of malevolent spirits. This influence is seen in what are called Goinkhangs, which are reserved for the inmates of the demonic world. A Goinkhang is usually a small, dark room in a lonely corner of a monastery, in the eerie gloom of which are hung huge skins and the teeth and nails of animals, as well as the remains of sacrificial victims or enemies along with their weapons and armor. The walls of the room are covered with paintings of the misshapen forms of demons, black magicians, witches, ferocious animals, and vultures. The atmosphere is typically Himalayan, for these people, after all, spend their lives under the shadows of the groaning and cracking sound of descending glaciers and of great avalanches tumbling from the mountains. The paintings are typically Himalayan, too: although Buddhist art in general had its terrifying figures, the artists of the Himalaya had great freedom to enlarge and improve upon this grotesque world. Paintings of terrifying gods are meant to strike terror—an emotion that, temporarily at least, thrusts a man outside of himself. The Buddhist concept of the cycle of births and deaths is enacted here in all its sorrow and

pain until finally it points the path of nirvana, or salvation.

In contrast to the Goinkhang is the serene, peaceful atmosphere inside the temple chapels that form the center of these monasteries. Paintings on the walls and ceilings of the chapels depict either Jatakas, scenes of events from Gautama Buddha's life, or portraits of Tantra gurus (Siddhas). The gurus were the most eminent esoteric personalities of medieval India, and they provide ideal links between Hindu and Buddhist Tantricism. The wall paintings are done either directly on the dry plaster—not, as Western frescoes are, in wet plaster—or upon canvas glued to the walls. The temple walls are also hung with cloth paintings and brilliant brocade banners. The focal point of the chapels is the altar, which holds large enthroned images of gilded stucco or brass. Incense burns at one side, and oil lamps provide the only light apart from a few small windows and the main door.

Because Tantric art is meant to serve a religious, rather than an aesthetic purpose, and because artists believed that they acquired spiritual merit by copying prototypes, the art has not greatly changed over the centuries. The emphasis is not on style but on iconography. The earliest known motif is the naked Siva prototype, with phallus erect, who sits in a Yoga posture. First seen in the Indus valley civilization of the third millennium B.C., its corollaries are the representation of fierce deities, the protector gods, who

are often portrayed with blue or black skin and set in furious scenes suitable to the deep-seated demonism that formed the Himalaya's aboriginal faith. Another characteristic motif is the ever-popular Mithuna, or lovers, sometimes in sexual embrace. Depicted in a variety of forms, these are known in Tibet as the "yab-yum," or mother-father couple. A third anthropomorphic theme is the human-animal configuration, in which the deity appears as half-human and half-animal. An ensemble of these cardinal motifs and several other subsidiary symbols popular in the Himalaya is the Wheel of Life. First seen in the Gupta-period painting at the Ajanta caves in India, the Wheel of Life sums up both pictorially and philosophically the Hindu and Buddhist view of life and the causes of human sorrow.

The religions and the art of the Himalaya are derived from those of northern and central India and remain closely allied to them, but the isolation—the geographical hardship and the grandeur of the area—have given the beliefs and the culture that expresses them a magnificence and mystery of their own. Like the hundreds of gods and goddesses of Hindu and Buddhist pantheons who aspire to the same divine ideals, these paintings express a rare unity in diversity. And the Himalaya's artists are still at work, painting as the Byzantine artists did, according to ancient precepts—blissfully unaware that history, as always, has rushed on ahead of them.

ntokha Monastery, Bhutan: Vairocana. 17th century

105

The Galsworthy Saga

His life, like his work, was the epitome of late Victorianism, and his novels about the Forsyte family won him a Nobel prize. But his heart was perhaps too often in the right place—for pity can be an artist's worst enemy

The Galsworthys gather with friends for a group portrait taken in front of a rented summer house in Scotland in the 1880's. John stands at far right beside his sister Mabel. His other sister, Lilian, stands second from left. His father sits, commandingly, at center.

"I do wish I had the gift of writing, I really think that it is the nicest way of making money going, only it isn't really the writing so much as the thoughts that one wants." Thus, seventy-six years ago, John Galsworthy first looked sideways at his literary future.

Not that he was, or would be, in any great need of money—always provided that he was willing to play the game according to the family rules. And the family, the Galsworthys, were in fact the Forsytes—so much so that one of his sisters begged him, in his own interests, not to publish the novel that was later to become the first volume of *The Forsyte Saga—The Man of Property*—or at any rate to publish it anonymously. But, he inquired ironically, which of the family did she suppose was likely to read it?

The Galsworthys had for centuries been small farmers and the like in south Devon. One of them, a merchant at Plymstock, sold out when his wife died, took his immense brood of children to London, and prospered in real estate during the great mid-Victorian expansion. His sons prospered, too.

Galsworthy's father became a lawyer

© 1967 *The Sunday Times*

but thought little of that dusty profession; he moved into finance, made a large fortune, which he reinvested in (of course) property, and over a considerable period of time had an annual income of some £12,000 a year. He was the original for Old Jolyon, the senior member of the Forsyte family in the Saga, who veiled "under a Jove-like serenity that perpetual antagonism deep-seated in the bosom of a director towards his shareholders." He was, his son wrote in a direct description, a tough, quick-tempered, lonely man with "a very strong vein of fastidiousness, and such essential deep love of domination, that he found, perhaps, few men of his own age and standing to whom he did not feel natively superior."

Although he loved children, at least, Galsworthy's father did not marry until he was forty-five. His wife, twenty years younger, came from a Midland family of small squires and industrialists. She was a woman of exquisite appearance, a good housekeeper, rider, and archer; she was also a rigid conformist with a knack for irritating her family to the point of frenzy by her mere presence in the room. She was

spectacularly jealous of her husband, whom she left when he was eighty-six on the grounds that he showed excessive interest in the governess of one of their grandchildren.

Nevertheless Galsworthy enjoyed an idyllic childhood in the contemporary smart stockbroker belt in the hills of Surrey, in the house that is the original of Robin Hill in the Saga.

He does not seem to have minded being sent away—first to a prep school at Bournemouth, then to Harrow. There, in what he later called "the mills of gentility," "we were debarred from any real interest in philosophy, history, art, literature and music, or any advancing notions in social life or politics." Like many another subsequently distinguished son of the Establishment—for example, Stanley Baldwin and Winston Churchill—he made no particular mark in the school.

He did, however, begin to turn into "something of a swell," a process he extended at New College, Oxford. Reading law, he took a second-class degree—a very respectable academic achievement—although he was at pains, in the English manner, to show no signs of effort. To all appearances he

By J. W. LAMBERT

spent his time strolling through the more fashionable streets of the university town, cultivating a "nonchalant and languid manner," playing walk-on parts for the university dramatic society (which was then regarded as deeply frivolous by the authorities), and becoming an expert on horse racing. Shortsighted in his right eye, he took to wearing an eyeglass (spectacles were reserved for use at home), cultivated a small group of suitably born friends, made a point of overspending his allowance, and habitually pawned his watch near the end of every term.

By the time he left the university his family had moved into one of a row of houses they had built on the edge of Regent's Park in London, and the Forsyte way of life was in full swing, if the phrase can be used of anything so fussily torpid. Reading for the Chancery Bar, going with the family to Switzerland or Scotland, young John dribbled the time away—put to shame, one might think, by his two sisters, one actively intellectual, the other intensely musical, and neither of them very Forsytean.

Suddenly, excitement arrived in the person of a rebellious young Bavarian painter who rather surprisingly was invited to live with the family. Both girls fell in love with him. In due course he married the intellectual one; the other took to good works of a musical nature (Harriet Cohen and Myra Hess were two of her protégées) and—although she did in real life achieve a perfectly satisfactory marriage—became the model for June Forsyte, who turned to good works after a disappointment in love. Young John himself was hardly less bowled over by his first contact with an artist, and at the same time he found his mind stirring under the influence of a remarkable schoolmaster's family, with one of whom, Ted Sanderson, he had been at Harrow. His existence as a sort of stiff-necked Bertie Wooster was being gradually eroded.

But he was also, Wooster-wise, involved with a girl whom the family thought not at all the thing—she had no money and gave singing lessons for a living. A trip to Canada failed to dissolve this association, though Galsworthy himself wrote, "Nothing will ever come of this matter between me and Sybil, I am too vague, and she doesn't care."

Cunningly, his father now suggested that John's prospects would be better if he were to switch from the Chancery Bar to the Admiralty Division and that it would be a splendid idea if, in order to learn about the practical background of this sort of law, he were to take a long sea voyage. Along with Ted Sanderson he set off, via Ceylon and Australia, to visit Robert Louis Stevenson on Samoa. He never got there, because his companion came down with dysentery in the interior of Suva; Galsworthy now exhibited the remarkable talent for nursing that was later to be worked so hard. Coming home, they boarded a ship called the *Torrens* at Adelaide. The first mate, Galsworthy wrote home, "is a Pole called Conrad and is a capital chap, though queer to look at; he . . . has a fund of yarns." Joseph Conrad also had the unfinished manuscript of a story called "Almayer's Folly" in his cabin, but didn't mention it.

Back in London, his allowance increased to £350 a year, called to the bar if briefless, he moved out of the family house and shared a flat in Victoria Street with an Oxford friend. Gradually his mental horizons began to widen again. . . . "I do wish I had the gift of writing." The Sandersons' conversation kept him on the hop. Religion was much under discussion; the twenty-five-year-old Galsworthy was not a believer, but, he suggested, "The great thing, I take it, is to cultivate a stiff upper lip . . ."

More important, he suddenly began to notice what was under his nose in this world. And what he saw shocked yet fascinated him horribly. Almost the only service that his father required of him, apart from dancing attendance on the family, was that from time to time

he should act as rent collector. His duties took him to the poorer parts of London. He became almost obsessed with slum life. He describes himself at this time in a passage written nine years later in the novel *The Island Pharisees:*

The streets, in fact, after his long absence in the East, afforded him much food for thought—the curious smugness of the passers-by; the utterly unending bustle; the fearful medley of miserable, overdriven women, and full-fed men, with leering, bull-beef eyes . . . the appalling chaos of hard-eyed, capable dames with defiant clothes, and white-cheeked hunted-looking men; of splendid creatures in their cabs, and cadging creatures in their broken hats—the callousness and the monotony!

He visited flophouses, prowled the streets at night. He told his friends how appalling things were. They agreed— and asked, "Why don't you *do* something?"

But Galsworthy's concern with the suffering of others was occasioned more by the pain knowledge of it gave him than by the pain experience of it gave them: the sensitive liberal's situation in a nutshell—and at least an improvement on total insensibility. But once awakened in Galsworthy, this concern became altogether too powerful. It made, as it always does, for sentimentality. It accounts for the perceptive comment Ford Madox Ford made when he saw tears in Galsworthy's eyes on account of an anecdote about Turgenev and his peasant mistress: "suddenly I had of him a conception of a sort of frailty, as if he needed protection from the hard truths of the world. . . . The disease from which he suffered was pity . . ."

And pity, a form of self-indulgence, is an artist's worst enemy. Even at the turn of the century not all the poor were utterly miserable all the time, but one would never suppose otherwise on the strength of Galsworthy's works. Conrad, later, advised him to get more skepticism into his writing, and even went so far as to suggest that Galsworthy got a sadistic pleasure from de-

Ada Galsworthy, 1886

John Galsworthy, 1921

Margaret Morris, 1910

John Galsworthy's triangulated love life started with Ada, his cousin's wife, whom he married in 1905 only to fall in love five years later with a nineteen-year-old dancer named Margaret Morris. Their romance was consummated solely by kisses stolen in taxicabs.

scribing the sufferings of the weak and the unfortunate. Galsworthy himself knew all this perfectly well. He warned others against it. "Pity is tripe," he made one of his characters keep repeating to himself. But it was no good; in art as in life he remained a helpless victim of the soft touch.

He was also, though, a genuinely generous man, ready and eager to lay out his money in a good cause even if it had no vestige of sentimental appeal. He is said to have made a point of living on only half his (admittedly ample) income and of giving away the rest. Perhaps that was a sentimental gesture, too—or a kind of expiation for the source of the tainted money that he collected from the slums.

*B*efore long the full force of his emotional attention was to be violently deflected. In the course of the interminable round of family visits, just before he set off on his travels, he had met the new wife of a cousin, Arthur Galsworthy. This young woman, of dark, strong-featured, not to say haughty appearance, had in fact accompanied him in a song, for she was a first-class pianist. And that was that; but on his return his sisters began pouring out to him in stricken accents appalling tales of the nightmare time poor Ada was going through with Arthur, who was represented as a drunken brute. More frightful suffering—and in his own class, too!

Ada was the daughter of a most ec-

centric Norwich gynecologist who built himself a mausoleum and used to spend his Sundays sitting and gazing at it, puffing a clay pipe. When he took possession of his tomb, Ada moved to London with her mother and then set out on what can only be called a husband-trawling tour of Europe. Despite her talent at the piano, it was some years before Arthur Galsworthy was hooked at Biarritz and the couple settled in London.

Why she married him, unless merely to escape from the sordid round of luxury bargain-hunting (and he was, after all, an Old Etonian with great expectations), is far from clear. What is clear is that, her own statements apart, there is absolutely no evidence to support the picture of Arthur as a fiend in human shape and plenty to suggest that he was in fact a mild and moderate man. Even so, there was perhaps little hope of the marriage being a close one. Their sexual relationship was not a success; they were not, as he was later to put it, "on terms," though it seems deeply improbable that he ever actually raped her, as Soames Forsyte was made to rape his wife Irene in *The Man of Property*. He did not care for music, and she was understandably remote from his only real interests, the volunteer Yeomanry and bridge.

When Ada and John met again— over pigeon pie at the annual cricket match between Eton and Harrow—he must have seen her with new eyes. Pity, this time, was indeed akin to love.

Further meetings followed. Then, at Easter, 1895, Ada and her mother went to Monte Carlo for a holiday— and John came, too. There, on a hotel terrace beside the Mediterranean, a long look was exchanged, and all was admitted.

Intense sexual passion, Galsworthy leads us to suppose, flared up between them. Six months later, after much painful restraint, they became lovers. And before that something ultimately much more important had happened. At the bookstall at the Gare du Nord in Paris, on the way home, Ada said to John, "Why don't you write?"

His own faint inclinations thus reinforced by the woman he loved, he set about doing so; and she then devoted herself to making him into a writer and keeping him going, with unremitting zest. He never had to have (or perhaps was not allowed) a secretary; Ada took dictation and typed and retyped down the years. And since, in book after book, Galsworthy returned to the theme of the woman tied to an unloved husband, it is not unreasonable to suppose that she gave him some hints as to what it was like.

Galsworthy started by trying to imitate Bret Harte and Kipling. His first story, "Dick Denver's Idea," concerned an American gambler's picturesque method (involving a duel in a cave) of ridding a woman of a brute of a husband. In another a couple ended a month of stolen bliss by dying in each other's arms when their carriage, bearing them back "to prison—to prison—to prison," collided with a train. Freud would have had no trouble with these fantasies; but a literary talent-spotter might have been excused for overlooking their author when they were published—at Galsworthy's expense and under the name John Sinjohn—in 1897.

Only Ada's eye of faith saw their promise. The pair were now meeting regularly in London. Nobody knew but Galsworthy's sisters—and, most probably, Ada's mother. But his Campden Hill studio—where he slept, perhaps they both slept, on a camp bed covered with furs from animals he had shot on his travels, alongside a Turkish bath cabinet installed for his rheumatism—was not their only meeting place; they even found it possible to go away together. Arthur was often busy with his Yeomanry.

But why did they conceal things at all? Because of the pain a scandal would cause their families? Yes, up to a point. Even when the blissful period of Arthur's absence at the Boer War was coming to a close with his return and she positively left him, neither they nor he did anything about getting a divorce. It seems impossible to avoid the miserable conclusion that these two men—one forty, the other thirty-four—were unwilling to hazard their allowances and possibly their inheritances, should their fathers turn ugly (as Galsworthy was to make Old Jolyon turn for so long against young Jolyon, the family aesthete who, unlike his creator, did sacrifice his patrimony to live openly with the woman he loved).

Much as we must admire independence, there are probably few of us who would exercise it in similar circumstances. Right or wrong, Galsworthy *was* willing to play the game according to the family rules. If he had not been, he would never have become a writer; he wrote and published for ten years before ever making a penny from his work—or particularly deserving to, for his craft developed slowly, the comic irony that is still his strongest point only gradually coming to infiltrate the florid melodrama.

*L*ittle by little, mostly through his old friend Conrad—who was by now settled in England and had already developed a reputation among intellectuals—Galsworthy was making acquaintances in literary London. He was also trying to forgive Edward Garnett, fictional midwife par excellence, for saying in a publisher's reader's report that this writer would never be an artist but would always see life as from the windows of a club. (Garnett performed the same service for many British writers, including D. H. Lawrence as well as Conrad and Galsworthy, as in the United States Maxwell Perkins was to do even more drastically for Thomas Wolfe.) Later, when they had become close friends and Galsworthy relied heavily on his advice, Garnett got into trouble again for saying that the novelist shouldn't have tried to write about aristocrats because he didn't know enough. Galsworthy "knocked me off my length," as Garnett put it, in a metaphor all too suitably drawn from the game of cricket, "by sending me a list of 130 upper-class men and women he had met or known."

Galsworthy tried to escape from the clubman's image by impersonating, in his picaresque satirical novel *The Island Pharisees*, a young Belgian beatnik he had met, an embittered wanderer never at a loss for a gibe at the established. It was no good; he kept the offbeat character but made the central figure a young man like himself. The latter was a mouthpiece, certainly, for an all-out attack on the ugliness of the big cities, the horror of the slums from which his own family drew much of its money, the willful blindness, the sexual hypocrisy, he found everywhere; but he was also irredeemably locked in the comfortable world of gentlemen's clubs, grand town mansions, and spacious, tranquil country houses blandly belonging to that upper-middle-class society that was so cruelly confining, then shunning, his Ada.

The novel was several times rejected, until on Conrad's recommendation the publisher Heinemann accepted it. (Conrad, at this time, was writing Galsworthy fulsome letters, telling friends that the stuff wasn't much good, but working hard to push it in the market. Since Conrad's books made him no money in spite of his reputation, perhaps he was inclined to this ambiguous course by an awareness that Galsworthy was both rich and notoriously generous). When *The Island Pharisees* was published in 1904, it met with a dim reception. Galsworthy later wrote a ruefully comic story about an author whose friends praise him but who attracts no readers, and who ends up by boring even himself.

But now, at last, his father died. His inheritance safe, he went off publicly with Ada to the Dartmoor farm that became one of their homes and in effect challenged Arthur to get a divorce, which he did. Meanwhile, Galsworthy, who by this time and for the rest of his life never failed to write steadily for several hours a day, had resigned from his club and embarked upon *The Man of Property*.

In this novel's brilliant opening chapter—one could almost say "scene," so dramatically is it composed—the rich, overstuffed Forsyte family is spread before us at a party given to celebrate young June's engagement to the architect Philip Bosinney—an engagement to be brought to nothing by his entanglement with the equivocal Irene, Soames Forsyte's wife. And Soames is the man of property: business, buildings, paintings, wife—all, to him, are a matter of possession. This is his strength—as it was the strength of Victorian England; and it is his weakness—as it was the weakness of Victorian England. For he could not, in all sincerity, understand any of the warmer human feelings, just as England was pained and puzzled by the aspirations of its subject races. First in *The Man of Property*, then in succeeding volumes of the Saga, we watch ironclad loneliness being undermined until a sort of frosty tranquillity is reached.

The gestation of *The Man of Property* was followed by fearful birth pains. Galsworthy was always eager for other people's advice, agitated when he got it, but usually willing in the end to act upon it. His wife, his sisters, Conrad, Ford Madox Ford, Gilbert Murray, Garnett—suggestions came from all over. But it was Garnett again who caused the trouble with *The Man of Property*. In the original manuscript Bosinney was made to commit suicide when he learned that Soames had forcibly asserted his marital rights upon Irene. Garnett said this was absurd; Galsworthy asked Garnett to come to Italy at the author's expense; Garnett replied that he'd rather not visit them until John and Ada were married. Galsworthy fretted and in the end compromised by leaving us in the dark as to whether Bosinney stepped under the bus on purpose or not. With the publishing of this book, in 1906, Galsworthy made his mark, though initially it sold only about five thousand copies.

His real reputation was made by a success in the theatre. In the same year *The Silver Box*, sharply pointing up the fact that there is one law for the rich and another for the poor, was produced. After this double success, there was no stopping Galsworthy.

Novels satirizing the upper classes, plays exposing social evils, poured out steadily, though Galsworthy was not to return to the Forsytes until after the First World War. (The other novels in the Forsyte trilogy, *In Chancery* and *To Let*, were published in 1920 and 1921.) But one novel, *The Dark Flower* (1913), was notably out of key with the rest of his torrential output; it was a burningly personal tale, with no social or humanitarian content, about a man sadly torn between the onset of passion for one woman and the giving of pain to another.

Galsworthy had eventually felt able to marry Ada in 1905 (very soon after the death of his father and the safe accession of his inheritance). But five years later, forty-three years old and very famous, at least as a dramatist, he met in the Savoy Theatre, London, a nineteen-year-old artist-dancer, Margaret Morris. A pupil of Isadora Duncan's brother Raymond, she had designed the sets and costumes, and trained the actors in "Greek positions," for a production of Gluck's *Orfeo*, one of Galsworthy's two favorite operas (the other was *Carmen*). She was asked to lunch with the Galsworthys, and what at first seemed to her an idyllic relationship developed between the three of them. She was helped to start a school of movement and given a part in a new Galsworthy play.

True, "My love for John grew daily and I gloried in it." But she knew how devoted he and Ada were and "was at great pains not to show my feelings." I quote from her entirely credible and delightful memoir, *My Galsworthy Story*. And then, she goes on, "I had the shock of my life when he took me to dinner . . . one evening and suddenly leant across the table to ask: 'Have you ever been in love?'"

The next day, in a taxi, after a visit to a theatrical costumers, she "snuggled up against him"—it was a very cold day; not surprisingly he kissed her. And afterward, "it was always like that, because John would only kiss me in the safety and seclusion of a taxi." Then he took to visiting her in her flat—solely, it appears, because he felt they should not be seen together often in restaurants. And there they sat, half paralyzed by desire, which Miss Morris calls emotion, and he protested that he was much too old for her, and she said they must not hurt Ada.

But Ada knew, and broke down before John. Margaret wrote her a letter full of self-reproach. Ada sent a masterly reply:

My dear Margaret,
    Thank you for your brave letter. You must not be unhappy, but very happy—first love at your age—can there be anything more holy! And you must not think of me —I am content. Just at present physical weakness dominates me and makes a bad impression, but the spirit is well-meaning and strong. . . .

And Margaret, of course, felt worse than ever. So did John. And so an old story was told again, as he gradually saw her less, wrote less, and finally got the affair out of his system by writing *The Dark Flower*.

Ada had won; but she now embarked with, so to speak, redoubled vigor upon her expert course of well-timed hypochondria—rheumatism, asthma, and frightful "colds"—which lasted until Galsworthy's death. And no sooner had she so successfully exercised her magnanimity toward this dazzled young woman than she embarked on a policy of perpetual motion that kept them both traveling—though he disliked it and she was too ill for it. In Spain, as soon as John showed his enthusiasm for the gypsy dancers, Ada became very unwell and needed his constant attention—reading *Travels with a Donkey* to her, getting her hot milk. In fact, as the years went by, Ada became steadily more possessive and self-centered; and with Galsworthy's last illness upon him, she laughed at his clumsiness when others could see that he was losing control. No wonder John wrote at one point, "This is what comes of giving of yourself to a woman body and soul. A. paralyzes me and has always paralyzed me."

This gloomy reflection occurred to him during the First World War. The arrival of this cataclysm hit him hard; well over military age at forty-seven, he speculated miserably over whether, had he been younger, he would have enlisted or been a conscientious objector, coming to the conclusion that he probably would not have joined up but would have been ashamed of himself in consequence. (Cousin Arthur was back in the army at fifty-four.) He was much upset when his mare was called up, and much relieved when she was rejected as unfit. Later on he and Ada did their bit by spending three months at a French hospital. In preparation Galsworthy took lessons in massage (while Ada designed a uniform that she was not allowed to wear), and throughout the winter of 1916–17 he massaged damaged soldiers for some five hours a day.

But for the most part he became what Ada rightly called an "appeals writer par excellence." The task came easily to him, for he had already for five or six years been an actively campaigning reformer. When the theatre critic of the London *Times* said of *Strife*, his play about industrial relations, "he has done much more than write a play, he has rendered a public service," he struck a congenial note.

The list of good causes—wartime issues apart—that Galsworthy championed is long and various, including not only divorce law reform but House of Lords reform (advocating life peerage), theatre censorship reform, minimum wages in sweated industries, woman suffrage, slum clearance, keeping children off the stage, help for prostitutes and for coal-pit ponies, the introduction of an averaging system for income tax, and, with great success, the modification of the imposition of solitary confinement.

*B*ut there were limits. Galsworthy would not, for example, join an appeal for the abolition of capital punishment. He himself was always perfectly well aware of what later came as an unpleasant surprise to many of his radical admirers—that though he wished to make the world a better place, he did not wish to make it a different one. He had acquired in some quarters, he noted, "the reputation of a revolutionary—a quaint conceit," adding that "the constant endeavor of his pen has merely been to show Society that it has had luck; and, if those who have had luck behave as if they knew it, the chances of revolution would sink to zero."

Besides, he wished to emphasize quite another aspect of himself as a writer:

I've neither the method nor the qualities of a social critic. I've only detachment in so far as I can examine *myself* in contact with life ... [my books are] simply the criticism of one half of myself by the other half ... there's quite enough of the dried-caste authority element in me to be legitimate subjects for the attack of my other half ... [my works are] not a piece of social criticism—they none of them are. If anything, a bit of spiritual examination.

As with the world at large, so with his own world, which was the world of the Forsytes. When carrying the story on to the postwar world in the three volumes of *A Modern Comedy*—with

Galsworthy sits with Ada, above, in an Arizona wood on one of the many trips he took for the sake of his ailing wife.

much interpolated sermonizing—he inevitably looked back to a more stable universe, though not, to be fair, in any Blimpish spirit. He was able, when he came to write about the 1920's, to describe without bitterness or self-righteousness the younger Forsytes' mobility within marriage, so different from the rigid social bonds that had controlled his own life and Ada's.

Despised by the younger literary world, Galsworthy lived majestically on. He refused a knighthood in 1918, though it was inadvertently announced, so that his refusal had to be announced as well. "Literature is its own reward," he absurdly told a reporter. But other honors were showered upon him; degrees and doctorates fell as thick as autumn leaves, the Order of Merit was followed by the Nobel prize. His acceptance speech was composed virtually on his deathbed:

I have made a sort of world with my pen, but has it any resemblance to the world we live in, either in England or anywhere else? ... It would be as true to judge France by the pictures of Maupassant, or Russia by the pen pictures of Turgenev, as to judge England by my pen pictures. We have all three been exiles all our days. ... I regret more than anything that I am barred—by temperament, habits of life, possessions—from the complete flow of sympathy. ...

That must be the cry of the artist always. Galsworthy was not one of the greatest. But he did indeed make a world with his pen. What C. E. Montague called his "almost disconcerting equity," the very understanding that enabled him to create that world, upset the new generation, who seemed to think that his identification with the Forsytes meant that he could not be a good novelist. But time is steadily making nonsense of Virginia Woolf's dismissal of him, along with H. G. Wells and Arnold Bennett, as one of those novelists who "write of unimportant things ... spend immense skill and immense industry making the trivial and the transitory appear the true and the enduring," and from whose novels "life escapes."

From Galsworthy's best work life has patently not escaped. The Forsyte stock lives in his pages, with "gray unmoving eyes hiding their instinct with its hidden roots of violence, their instinct for possession ..." Galsworthy knew it, felt it in his bones, filled it with the extraordinary pulse of sexual energy that drums through all his best work, recorded it from an ironic distance (at a dance, "the chaperones silting up along the wall," the young men "armored in professional gaiety," young Jolyon grasping, "as every artist should, at anything that might delay for a moment the effort of his work," the lady with "that fussy simpleness of dress which indicates the right to meddle").

He understood that Forsyte "instinct for possession" and balanced it perhaps with an instinct to be possessed.

He came to know that in the postwar world there was little place for the Forsytes. In our own there is less still —the tribal Forsytes have been displaced by the nonhereditary organization men of the managerial revolution, who must make do with luxury in place of property. There was something Roman about those bleak yet vital Victorians of Galsworthy's. If he needs a modest epitaph—well, he was the noblest Forsyte of them all.

J. W. Lambert, who lives in London, is literary editor of The Sunday Times.

GALLERIA DORIA PAMPHILI, ROME

Lionized in England, Newton appears in an allegorical painting of 1787 with Britannia and one of his young disciples.

by those words I anywhere take upon me to define the kind, or the manner of any action, the causes or the physical reason thereof, or that I attribute forces, in a true and physical sense, to certain centres (which are only mathematical points); when at any time I happen to speak of centres as attracting, or as endued with attractive powers." And again, "I here design only to give a mathematical notion of those forces, without considering their physical causes and seats."

What, then, is "force" if it is not a physical cause? To this question Newton's revolutionary answer is this: force is the "efficacy" of a cause unspecified and unknown. It is the mathematical measure of the strength of whatever unknown cause it is "that propagates it." The gravitational force does not cause a planet to move toward the sun. It is the *measure* of the strength of whatever it is that causes this motion. Though the cause of this force (and other forces) is unknown, forces themselves can be determined exactly, and this is all that philosophy requires. The force of a cause can be determined, in fact, by the three laws of motion. As the first law states, a body moves naturally in a straight line at uniform speed. Therefore, by this

law, when the uniform motion is changed in any way, we know that some cause is operating on that body. The strength, or force, of that cause is measured by the *amount* of change the cause induces, or more strictly, by the amount of acceleration the cause induces in a body of a given mass. As to the explanation of the gravitational force, says Newton, he has not been able to discover it empirically "and I frame no hypotheses. . . . To us it is enough that gravity does really exist, and act according to the laws which we have explained, and abundantly serves to account for all the motions of the celestial bodies, and of our sea."

"To us it is enough." With that regal pronouncement Newton summed up the meaning of his revolution in natural philosophy. Just as he had expected, philosophers like Huygens declared that the *Principia* was incomplete. For all the book's grandeur, they said, its author had failed to give a mechanical explanation of his gravitational force. It may be true, they argued, that planets move toward the sun in accordance with Newton's law, but surely natural philosophy must explain why they do so in terms of the material push that must propel them. Newton had said that forces measure causes unknown, but why should philosophers leave these causes unknown? Such a question is not really answerable, and Newton's reply —it cannot be called an argument— was simply: "To us it is enough." He, Newton, was satisfied. Beyond such concepts as he had laid down—beyond force, mass, and acceleration—philosophy could not go without dribbling away into vain speculation no whit superior to the old philosophy.

"The whole burden of philosophy seems to consist in this—from the phenomena of motions to investigate the forces of nature, and then from these forces to demonstrate the other phenomena." Indeed, he suggested with truly prophetic intuition, there are probably other forces like gravity that operate in nature. "Have not small

particles of Bodies certain Powers, Virtues, or Forces by which they act at a distance . . . for producing a great part of the Phenomena of Nature?" If so, philosophers must investigate them and find the laws governing their operation, just as he, Newton, had investigated the force of gravitation by way of example of his mathematical method.

There was no way for Newton to prove that the "whole burden of philosophy" was one thing and not another. In brief time, however, men came to agree with him. He conquered, not by force of argument, but by the overwhelming power of his peerless example: the *Principia Mathematica* itself. If, as Newton said, the law of gravitation is but a sample of his "mathematical way," then men agreed that science need go no farther than Newton had already gone. Forces may measure causes unknown, but Newton's new mathematical science of forces was more comprehensive, more precise, and more rigorous than anything natural philosophy had ever seen before. It was also freer; for Newton's belief was not a shackle but a liberation, and that liberation is what distinguishes modern science from all previous philosophies.

The modern scientist, disciple of Newton, does not ask what causes a force, or what energy is, or how charged particles can attract each other. It is enough for scientists that concepts like force or energy be mathematically precise, derivable from experiment, and capable of explanation according to Newtonian standards of precision. What metaphysicians might say—what "reason" might demand—is of little concern to scientists; they have been freed by Newton's *Principia* to comprehend nature without deciding once and for all what nature ultimately is.

This was exactly how Newton wanted it to turn out, though his reasons were only partly scientific and only partly revealed. The truth was that he himself had no doubt about the mysterious unknown cause that propagated the force of his system. It was God himself, "incorporeal, living, intelligent, omnipresent," though Newton never dared say so outright. He could only hope that men might follow his example and cease to arrogate to matter what properly belonged to God. Ironically, the mathematical method, through which science won its freedom, was the means by which Newton hoped to preserve God's place as ruler and sustainer of his creation. Like Janus, he faced two ways—toward the science of the future and the faith of the past.

Newton was forty-four when the *Principia* appeared. He had forty more years to live and to enjoy his fame, which grew more immense with each passing year until in time he found himself being looked upon as a kind of semideity. Honors and emoluments came one by one, but too slowly in the first few years to prevent Newton's suffering a nervous breakdown, during which he wildly accused John Locke of "embroiling" him with women. Shortly afterward he begged Locke, like a child, to forgive him. Then his iron pose of aloofness cloaked him once more and did so until the end of his life.

In 1696 Newton's admirers obtained for him the very crown of his ambition: an honorable post in His Majesty's government. He was named first Warden, and later Master, of the Mint. With that appointment Newton packed up and left Cambridge and never looked back. The institution that had housed and sustained him for thirty-five years he now left behind as if it were a wretched village and he a young man burning to try the metropolis. He bought a handsome house in London, rode in a coach, and entertained splendidly. In 1703, when Hooke died, he condescended to become President of the Royal Society. In 1705 he was knighted by Queen Anne, and in an official pedigree he feigned the hypothesis that he was a gentleman by birth as well as merit. He became a favorite of the court and an acquaintance of the celebrated, who hung on his words—which were as few and as final as ever. Except for revising the *Principia* and publishing his early work in optics, he all but abandoned science. Once, when Continental mathematicians sent him a problem to be solved, Newton exploded in rage. "I do not love to be printed upon every occasion much less to be dunned and teezed by foreigners about Mathematical things or to be thought by our own people to be *trifling* away my time about them when I should be about ye King's business." No doubt it irked him to be taken still for a mere mathematician instead of a man of the world.

To amuse himself, Newton delved deeply into the kind of crabbed erudition that was already growing old-fashioned. As his avocation for thirty years, he worked on a chronology that would co-ordinate the events in ancient pagan history with the events in basic history, namely the historical narrative of the Bible. He worked, too, to decipher such prophetic symbols as the seven vials and the seven trumpets and hoped that by translating the Biblical term "magi" into its proper meaning of "cheats and liars" he might infer post-Biblical history from prophetic Biblical texts. A skeptical Frenchman explained such scholarly aberrations in the great man by supposing that he had never recovered from his nervous breakdown. This was not true, yet it must be said there *was* something amiss with Newton in spite of his fame and his prosperity. Men noticed the glazed look in his eye and his curious inattention even in the midst of the bright society that he had longed for during his years at Cambridge. By now, his days of "thinking unto the problem" were over; perhaps he realized they were better days than he had ever thought. He seemed, at any rate, estranged and homeless. Once, late in his life, there was a gathering of Lincolnshire men at a London tavern, and upstairs, where the gentry mingled, a guest was told that a certain odd figure was sitting downstairs among the commoners. The man came down and found the aged Sir Isaac sitting among the sons of Lincolnshire plowmen, quite silent, but apparently content; Woolsthorpe's "sober, silent, thinking lad" momentarily at peace.

Doubtless Newton's heart was not in the age in which he now lived and which looked upon him as its special hero. Infidelity and skepticism seemed to be rising. There were signs that his own grand vindication of God's providence might prove futile in the end. Eager Newtonians were coming to conceive of gravity as an inherent property of matter and so were resuscitating materialism in a new, Newtonian form. He was an old man by now, and he felt urgently the need to set his faith upon lasting foundations. He sat down to write what he called "A Short Scheme of the True Religion," a set of propositions that would both contain the essence of religion and yet withstand skeptical assault. He wrote it once, then a second time; then again, and then twice more. He could not get it right. The true religion evaded him, just as infidelity was evading his titanic effort to forestall it.

In the year 1727, at the age of eighty-four, Newton died, and six peers of the realm carried his coffin to Westminster Abbey. With his quaint Biblical prophecies and his Hebraic God he was by then something of a relic; for a skeptical, experimental generation was rising, and it was out of spirit with his deepest concerns. By a curious irony, historians have sometimes called this dawning era the Newtonian Age.

Walter Karp, essayist and biographer, is a Contributing Editor to HORIZON. *His most recent book is* Charles Darwin and the Origin of Species, *published in the* HORIZON *Caravel series.*

Ancient Aches and Pains

The ills of ancient man, traced in his bones and art, tell us how he lived and died and link his world to ours

Disease never comes haphazardly. It always reflects the circumstances of our lives. Dental decay, cancer of the lung, tennis elbow, coronary thrombosis, beriberi, and innumerable other ailments are very precise indicators of the things we use, eat, do, or lack. This holds true for creatures other than modern man. Fossil sea urchins millions of years old bear the tooth marks of animals that took a snap at them. Dinosaurs developed arthritis from chronic stress and strain, and primeval trilobites fell victim to bacterial infection. The bones of ancient men often preserve a record of injury or affliction that reveals how these people lived, what they ate and wore, what weapons they used, and even what kind of society they lived in. The study of ancient disease and injury is called palaeopathology, and it has much to say about life in antiquity and in more recent times as well.

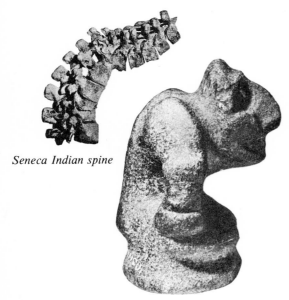

Seneca Indian spine

San Domingo hunchback

Not all the evidence is in bones. Ancient ailments have often been faithfully recorded in works of art. Sometimes the skeletal evidence supplements the artistic. For example, no one really knows whether American Indians were afflicted with tuberculosis before 1492 or whether the Europeans imported the disease. Tuberculosis of the vertebrae, or Pott's disease, produces hunchbacks, and many hunchbacked spines have been found in the New World. The one at left below belonged to a Seneca Indian of around the thirteenth century A.D. Pott's disease probably caused the deformation, though other infections could conceivably have had the same result. But the fact that figurines of hunchbacks, all quite similar, are frequently found among American Indians is evidence that the deformity was widespread, and it is probable that tuberculosis was responsible. The hunchbacked figurine shown on this page is from San Domingo. It was used to pound grain.

From the nameless hordes of ancient cadavers a famous man is sometimes lifted from his sepulcher to be examined by the palaeopathologist. Tamerlane is such a case. This Mongol conqueror, whose name means simply "Timur the Lame," died in 1405. When the Gur Amir Mausoleum in Samarkand was opened in 1941, the remains were identified as Tamerlane's by the extensive tubercular destruction of the right thigh and shin bones and by the bony union that had immobilized his knee joint and his right arm. The historical record was thus confirmed, but the old tradition that he was an albino was refuted. The parts of his beard that had survived were a graying chestnut color.

Apart from solving such minor historical puzzles as this, the chief interest of the palaeopathologist is in what he can learn about ancient society. The bronze figure of the dwarf below is from Benin in West Africa. One of several beautiful and serious studies of dwarfism from Benin, it shows an achondroplastic dwarf, the kind seen in circuses and in the canvases of Velásquez. This sympathetic portrayal is a clear indication of a kindly attitude toward dwarfs, in a society where deformed children were usually regarded as bewitched. In ancient Egypt dwarfs seem to have been regarded with the same mixture of respect and affection. They also were allowed to take their place in society, as this limestone statue of 2500 B.C. makes clear. It shows a dwarf called Seneb with his wife and children, who are all of normal size.

West African dwarf

By CALVIN WELLS

An Egyptian dwarf and his family

The evidence of disease

Facial palsy caused by stroke has been deliberately and vividly portrayed, particularly in the arts of Africa and Peru, and there is no doubt that this ailment is an old one. Anthropomorphic vases are common in the arts of ancient Peru, and the asymmetrical features of the Mochica vase below surely reflect a deliberate attempt to re-create the lopsided expression of a sufferer from cranial hemorrhage or some other paralyzing lesion. The wooden dance mask at right, from Liberia, is a most accurate picture of what happens to a face that is paralyzed on one side.

A disease that has always been rare, yet was occasionally portrayed in the ancient world, is acromegaly. It is a pituitary abnormality that produces a thickened, bulbous nose, coarse lips, prominent brow ridges, and great elongation of the jaw. The hands and feet of the sufferer sometimes enlarge, and his personality may undergo changes. The pharaoh Akhenaten undoubtedly had some such pituitary malfunction. The portrait opposite, which dates from about 1365 B.C., clearly emphasizes the exceptional length of his lower jaw.

Later rulers of Egypt were also afflicted with acromegaly. The Ptolemies were Macedonian Greeks who ruled Egypt from the conquest of Alexander in 323 B.C. until the death of Cleopatra in 30 B.C. From their portrait coins, as well as from the historical record, we can see that for

Wooden dance mask from Liberia

three hundred years this intensely inbred family repeatedly produced persons with this disorder. Ptolemy I Soter, the first of the line, had prominent brow ridges, an enlarged nose and lips, and a heavy, jutting jaw, all realistically reproduced on the coin opposite. The nicknames of later rulers hint at abnormalities. A grandson of Ptolemy VI Philometer became Antiochus VIII of Syria. Does his nickname, Grypus, "hooknose," mean that he, too, was a victim of acromegaly? His brother was called Physkon, "the sausage," which was perhaps a reference to the obesity caused by endocrine malfunction.

Another glandular disorder that shows up in art is goiter, an enlargement of the thyroid gland. Some forms of it are closely linked to environmental factors, especially the chemistry of the available drinking water, and Pliny the Elder was only one of several classical writers to observe that certain localities had a high incidence of the disease. Greece and Asia Minor were two of these, and the coins of many of the major cities—Corinth, Seleucia, Athens—occasionally show a ruler with a swollen neck. In Africa the disease also appears. The carving opposite, from the Babwende tribe of the lower Congo, is an accurate representation of goiter. The Mochica pottery jug, from the Chicama valley in Peru, takes the form of a very dumpy little boy. It may also represent some form of thyroid or pituitary malfunction.

Mochica vase from Peru

Ptolemy I Soter, ruler of Egypt

The Pharaoh Akhenaten

Mochica pottery jug

Congolese carving

Mochica vase

Wooden mask from Nigeria

Mochica portrait vase

Queen of the land of Punt

What flesh is heir to...

What people wore, or didn't wear, is often detectable from their skeletons. The early Saxons apparently wore some sort of tightly laced buskin, for evidence of inflammation is frequently found on their shinbones. Misshapen toe bones are one of the commoner skeletal defects of our own day—usually traceable to the vanity of squeezing a size seven foot into a size five shoe. Such defects are occasionally found in Saxon foot bones, so we can assume that they, too, must have worn tight boots at times. By contrast, foot defects rarely occur among the dynastic Egyptians, presumably because they habitually went barefoot. The Mochica Indian shown on the vase above also went barefoot, but with less happy results. Parasites have invaded the soles

of his feet, causing severe infection.

Another form of infection that was, and is, common in Africa and South America is trachoma, which causes blindness. The wooden mask at the top of the page, from Nigeria, is used in a mime. It shows a blind man trying to find his mouth with a stick. A carving like this leaves no doubt about the emotional impact of such an abnormality on the people who observe it. The Mochica vase below it has also been given an expressive blind face.

The queen of the land of Punt, above right, is surely suffering from something, but palaeopathologists have not been able to agree on a diagnosis. This relief, found in the temple of Queen Hatshepsut at Deir el-Bahri, depicts the reigning queen of a country that

Hatshepsut visited about 1500 B.C. A reasonable guess is that the lady had congenital dislocation of the hips, a condition that causes protruding buttocks.

The disease depicted on the opposite page is readily diagnosed. This Egyptian stela of the New Kingdom portrays a temple official named Ruma. The shriveling of his right leg was probably caused by poliomyelitis. His disability did not prevent him from rising to high estate, and he performs his priestly duties with serenity.

Disease is mankind's unwelcome companion. Surprisingly enough, in this great age of science and medical innovation, man is still heir to all the fleshly ills portrayed in these ancient works of art and—to some extent—to most of the diseases of his ancestors.

Ruma, the temple official

Amulets or case studies?

Artists of ancient Mexico seem almost to have been obsessed with illness. The figurines on this page, from the collection of Dr. Kurt Stavenhagen in Mexico City, are pre-Columbian grave offerings that describe medically interesting cases. The man clutching his neck is suffering from tuberculosis of the spine. The figure of a pregnant woman is one of many that show various stages of pregnancy and birth. A mother's concern for her sick child is movingly portrayed in clay. The Indians must have undergone the ravages of malnutrition: one of the two victims shown here is starving to death. In addition there were less tractable diseases. The skin lesions sustained by the unfortunate at far right are thought to illustrate the final phase of syphilis or cancer. The visored bed or stretcher may show a method of strapping down a violent patient. Were these figurines supposed to ward off disease? Probably not. From the accuracy of their detail they could have been used by doctors for teaching, diagnosis, and treatment. Similar diagnostic figures have long been used by Chinese physicians when treating modest women.

Calvin Wells, a palaeopathologist, is the author of Bones, Bodies, and Disease.

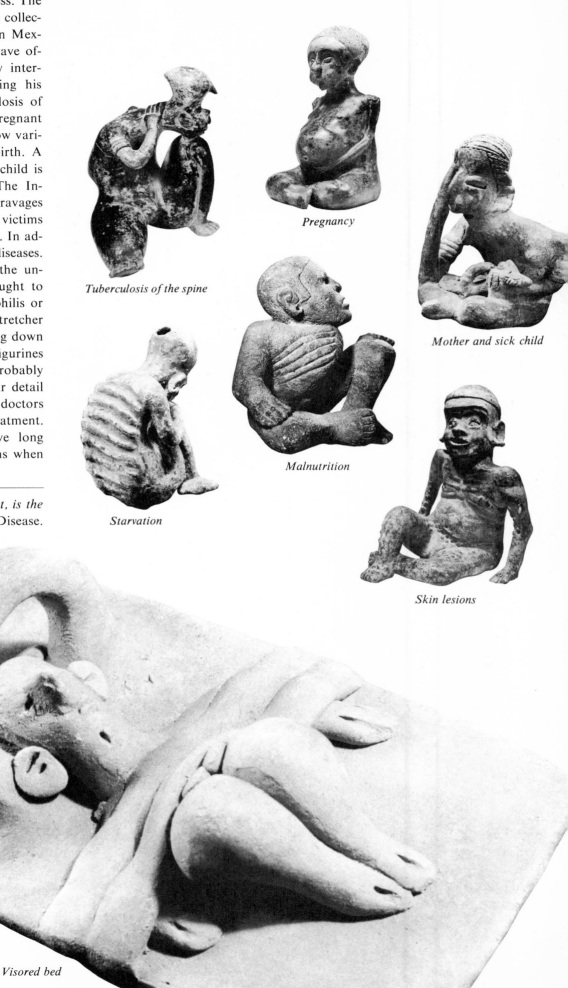

Tuberculosis of the spine

Pregnancy

Mother and sick child

Starvation

Malnutrition

Skin lesions

Visored bed